S0-ECL-390

Cures by Psychotherapy

RC
475.5
C 88
1984

Cures by Psychotherapy

What Effects Change?

Edited by
J. Martin Myers, M.D.

PRAEGER

PRAEGER SPECIAL STUDIES • PRAEGER SCIENTIFIC

New York • Philadelphia • Eastbourne, UK
Toronto • Hong Kong • Tokyo • Sydney

Library of Congress Cataloging in Publication Data
Main entry under title:

Cures by psychotherapy.

Papers presented at a recent (March 5-6, 1983)
conference sponsored by the Institute of Pennsylvania
Hospital in Philadelphia.
    Includes index.
    1. Psychotherapy — Congresses. I. Myers, J. Martin.
II. Institute of Pennsylvania Hospital.
RC475.5.C88 1984   616.89′14   83-21195
ISBN 0-03-069668-9

Published in 1984 by Praeger Publishers
CBS Educational and Professional Publishing
a Division of CBS Inc.
521 Fifth Avenue, New York, NY 10175 USA
©

All rights reserved

456789 052 987654321

Printed in the United States of America
on acid-free paper

Contributors

Paul Dewald, M.D.
Clinical Professor of Psychiatry
School of Medicine
St. Louis University
Medical Director
St. Louis Psychoanalytic Institute

Jerome D. Frank, M.D., Ph.D.
Professor Emeritus of Psychiatry
School of Medicine
Johns Hopkins University

Jerry M. Lewis, M.D.
Clinical Professor of Psychiatry
Family Practice and Community Medicine
Southwestern Medical School of the University of Texas at Dallas
Psychiatrist-in-Chief
Timberlawn Psychiatric Hospital

Robert Michels, M.D.
Barklie McKee Henry Professor and Chairman
Department of Psychiatry
Cornell University Medical College

Contributors

Paul H. Ornstein, M.D.
Professor of Psychiatry
College of Medicine
University of Cincinnati
Training and Supervising Psychoanalyst
Cincinnati Psychoanalytic Institute

Leon Salzman, M.D.
Professor of Clinical Psychiatry
Georgetown University Medical School
Past-President, American Academy of Psychoanalysis

Alan Z. Skolnikoff, M.D.
Associate Clinical Professor
Department of Psychiatry
University of California, San Francisco
Research Associate
Center for the Study of Neurosis
Langley Porter Psychiatric Institute

Preface

The goal of this book is to provide the practicing psychotherapist a pleasant way to learn what a small group of outstanding
psychiatrists believes brings about change in treatment and to enjoy
the debate they have in confronting one anothers' clinical beliefs.

Individual psychotherapy occupies a major part of the professional effort of from one to two hundred thousand persons in the
United States. Psychiatrists, psychologists, social workers, nurses,
and other mental health counselors are involved daily in one-to-one
psychotherapy with patients or clients in an attempt to bring about
some modification in the thinking, feeling, or behavior of the
patient. That change does come about – at least in a statistically
significant number of some groups – has been in recent years well
validated by clinical research.

A concern of great importance to all engaged in psychotherapy
is the process of psychotherapy itself. What is it that brings about
change? Various clinical groups and clinical individuals operate with
very different techniques and theoretical concepts about how to do
psychotherapy, what goes on in therapy, and with what effect. This
is so even if one considers only that large segment of psychotherapists who would characterize their type of psychotherapy as
"dynamic." The common element in dynamic psychotherapy is that
their various theoretical systems all include consideration of factors
that determine behavior but are outside the patient's immediate
awareness.

Clinical psychotherapists place different values on the importance of insight. They vary in their attitudes about how active the

therapist should be in advising, recommending, excusing, directing, educating, or revealing matters about their personal life or value systems, explicitly or implicitly. The clinicians who have an interest in the scientific understanding of their work or are looking for ways to be more effective in their practice are eager to know about these differences — whether they are important, which affect treatment, and with what group of patients.

As part of a Continuing Education Program it has been our pleasure for some years to look for and find topics about which clinical psychiatrists have a need and desire to learn more, and then to select a small group of outstanding persons to address the topic in an interactive way that has been both educational and fun for all those who participate. The format for interaction that seems to draw out the agreements and disagreements, the common ground and differences of the experts, is not serial paper presentations followed by discussion but the development of a continuing dialogue within the total faculty group. This is accomplished by paired presentations and round robin responses to the presentations. Then there develops a progressively better understanding of the congruences within the topic and a clearer differentiation of the individual position of each panelist. With a provocative and stimulating moderator this provides for greater spontaneity and understanding of each of the experts as a person in action.

To bring together a group of outstanding U.S. psychiatrists to discuss the hows and whys change comes about in psychotherapy appeared to be a very worthwhile project. The individuals invited were not only recognized as theoreticians but also as therapists engaged in active clinical work, so that clinical vignettes could be shared exemplifying their style of patient selection and treatment. All selected are "dynamic" psychotherapists with some psychoanalytic training but the group was not limited to orthodox Freudians. Representatives of those highly influenced by Sullivan and Kohut were included. As it becomes clear in the dialogues, each expert speaks for himself. For beginning orientation the reader is advised:

Dr. Paul Dewald is the representative most proximate to the centrum of present day psychoanalysis as it has evolved. Many readers may be surprised at what he has to say that so well signifies changes in the mainstream of psychoanalysis.

Dr. Jerome Frank is the elder statesman of the group and a pioneer in trying to fathom what it is in the wide diversities of psychotherapies that brings about change. He clearly identifies himself as not a psychoanalyst.

Dr. Jerry Lewis, psychoanalytically trained, has spent much of his productive career in investigating family dynamics, marital therapy, and psychotherapy education.

Dr. Robert Michels, the moderator and summarizer, has had broad psychiatric and psychoanalytic experience and responsibilities in academe.

Dr. Paul Ornstein is a psychoanalyst who has been one of Heinz Kohut's pupils and an exponent of his ideas.

Dr. Leon Salzman is a psychoanalyst trained also in Harry Stack Sullivan's Theory of Interpersonal Relations.

Dr. Alan Skolnikoff is a psychoanalyst who has worked closely with Mardi Horowitz, M.D. at the Clinical Research Center for the Study of Neuroses at Langley Porter Psychiatric Institute in San Francisco.

To make the reading of a book worthwhile it should be either educational or pleasurable. Because we believe that for the reader both the understanding of the issues and ideas and the excitement of the interaction is kept higher, the dialogues are in the words of the verbal interchanges rather than rewritten in journal prose. The sense of debate about differences and the humanness of reaction remain.

Many questions come up about what effects change in therapy. Some are answered; others are not. Our hope is that clinician readers will be stimulated to look more carefully at their own work with new ideas and perhaps thereby increase their skill.

Contents

Cures
by
Psychotherapy

Marital Therapy and Individual Change: Implications for a Theory of Cure

Jerry M. Lewis

Although the effectiveness of psychotherapy is not doubted by its participants and finds some support from controlled outcome studies, the issue of *how* psychotherapy works remains more a matter of belief than knowledge. In keeping with recent scientific paradigms, I assume that effective psychotherapy usually reflects the interaction of many variables and that different combinations of variables may account for therapeutic change in different patients. The variables are often categorized as patient, therapist, patient-therapist interaction, and "outside" variables, and each of these categories may contain a large number of discrete variables. In this presentation I wish to focus on one set of outside variables, marital and family factors, that may influence the effectiveness of individual psychotherapy.

I am not aware of published reports of psychotherapy research projects in which the role of marital or family variables is carefully scrutinized, nor do I have such data to present. Rather, I will argue that the sometimes striking changes in individuals resulting from marital or family therapy suggest that, in some instances, individuals may be so strongly "locked into" rigidly patterned interpersonal relationships that the course of their individual psychotherapy is decisively influenced. I am not arguing for the global superiority of one therapy or another, but that the success of such therapies, focusing specifically on repetitive, entrenched relationship patterns, can enrich the paradigms with which we attempt to understand the effectiveness of individual psychotherapy. Finally, I will review selectively an emerging, if controversial, body of theory that offers a conceptual bridge between individual change and interpersonal relationships.

As suggested above, marital and family variables are seldom emphasized in designing psychotherapy research projects and, I might add, are often unattended in clinical work with individual patients. Frank[1] is one of the exceptions in calling for closer attention to such variables, but it is instructive to note that the recent report of the American Psychiatric Association's Commission on Psychotherapies[2] pays scant attention to such factors.

A second reason for this focus is the recent work on Expressed Emotion (EE) and relapse from schizophrenia and depressive disorders.[3, 4, 5] Expressed Emotion is an index of hostile, critical intrusiveness by one or more family members towards patients recently discharged from psychiatric hospitals. Patients returning to high EE families have three to four times the relapse rate noted in patients returning to low EE families. An interaction between EE and psychotropic medication is suggested by the finding that although the high relapse rate of patients returning to high EE families can be lowered by appropriate medication, the lower relapse rate of patients returning to low EE families is not influenced by psychotropic medication.

Although these studies are not specifically concerned with psychotherapy and there is much to learn about EE and its interaction with psychotropic medication, it requires little imagination to suspect a comparable interaction between the effects of psychotherapy and marital or family variables.

A third reason for the focus on marital and family variables is personal. My psychotherapeutic practice, supervision, and teaching have, I suspect, been more or less typical for my generation of psychotherapists. My orientation is based primarily on psychoanalytic psychology, modified in recent years by interpersonal and existential constructs and when psychotherapy was successful it seemed related to a group of variables. These included: the development of a collaborative alliance, the facilitation of the patient's self-exploration, my capacity to alternate periods of effectively aroused closeness and more distant detachment, attention to both resistance and transference-countertransference phenomena, and a major reliance on a small cluster of traditional interventions.[6, 7]

This focus on the overt processes associated with effective psychotherapy avoided the question of how a psychotherapeutic interaction characterized by such processes led to change within the patient. The focus, however, allowed something of a comfortable sense of certainty that I knew what I was doing. Even this sense of understanding was shaken by my introduction to marital and family therapy, which grew out of an involvement in family system research rather than dissatisfaction with the results of individual psychotherapy. I began to experiment with marital and family therapy. As I learned from my work and that of others, I began to assess most clinical situations from the individual, marital, and family perspectives, and I selected interventions on the basis of which modality seemed to offer the greatest possibility of therapeutic effectiveness. The impact of successful marital or family therapy on individual functioning has led to a reconsideration of those factors that make human change possible. Let me illustrate with a clinical vignette chosen because of what appear to be successful results:

Mr. and Mrs. A. were both in their 60s when seen on seven occasions for marital therapy. Actually, however, I had known them both for many years. Mrs. A. had been in individual psychotherapy for many years with a colleague, and her treatment had, at times, involved lengthy periods of hospitalization. Her symptomatology included alcohol and barbiturate abuse, impulsivity, and a variety of severe depressive phenomena. Although her personality structure had many hysterical features, she was seen as having preoedipal psychopathology with a primitive and narcissistic core. In today's clinical language, her condition would be understood as a border-line personality organization.

I was asked to see her in consultation twice, once following a near-fatal attempted suicide and again for help with a severe transference fixation containing psychotic elements.

Mr. A. was a remote, compulsive, socially powerful man who had achieved great economic success. Although appearing attached to his wife, he seemed not at all psychologically oriented and refused to be involved in any form of treatment. At one stage of her hospital treatment I was asked to see him in consultation. He came reluc-tantly, and over the course of ten individual interviews remained pleasant, but distant and uninvolved. His view was that his wife had something wrong that needed fixing, and he would wait (stoically, I would add) until she was "fixed." Although he could share the facts of his own early, intense psychological deprivation, he could not approach underlying residual effects. We stopped our efforts at exploration at his insistence, delivered with polite finality.

Several years later he called and asked for help. He seemed desperate and said that he could no longer tolerate his wife's drink-ing, their increasingly enraged interactions, and his growing sense of hopelessness. During the past month she had withdrawn from individual psychotherapy and was being cared for by her internist who tried to control her use of both antianxiety and antidepressive medications. I suggested that both he and his wife come to see me.

During the first marital session Mr. A. initially maintained his detached focus on her behavior but with some encouragement began to share the feelings of impotence, anger, sadness, and growing hope-lessness that he had expressed during the telephone call. He cried openly and expressed his fear that he would die without ever having been really close to another person. Mrs. A. watched and listened with startled attention and, late in the interview, at my request, took his hand and quietly held it.

Their marital dynamics seemed based, in part, on their mutual fear of intimacy; he because of fears of abandonment and she because of fears of merger and loss of ego boundaries. The approach I selected was to attempt to assist them in negotiating a new balance of closeness and distance, keeping in mind the fragility of her ego and his rigid but faltering defensiveness. Several marital therapy techniques proved useful: The first involved structured exercises in communicating their needs to each other directly and clearly, particularly their affective messages. The second involved contingency contracting. When asked, for example, what her husband could do for her, Mrs. A. requested to be held for 30 seconds each day. Mr. A., obviously uncomfortable, wanted to know whether such holding was to occur in the standing, sitting, or recumbent position. He agreed, but when asked to counter with what he wanted in return from her, requested that she stop drinking. I told him that was asking for too much too soon and that he needed to make a more reasonable request. After some hesitation he asked that she not watch television during breakfast, for some years their only daily meal together.

They were seen again in two weeks, this time more relaxed with each other, but each articulating complaints about the other's failure to live up to their trade-off completely. He reported that she sometimes brought a portable radio to breakfast, and she indicated that when he put his arms around her, he kept his body at some distance. I assumed a role of a benign authority, always focusing on their disturbed interaction rather than their individual behaviors.

During the remaining sessions we negotiated a series of trade-offs, all of which shared the theme of cautiously diminishing the distance between them. These included her agreement to spend one day each week with him at their ranch in return for his spending two weeks every six months with her in Europe. Our final session concerned their sexual relationship. They had not had sexual intercourse in a number of years, and he feared he was impotent. They were given a number of suggestions in matter-of-fact language. They said they would call when they returned from their first European trip.

Several months later I received a jointly written note of appreciation in which each expressed how much better the other was. Four years later they came to discuss their concern about the depression they observed in a middle-aged son. At that time they reported the continuance of a satisfactory marital relationship. Mrs. A.'s behavior was markedly changed. She no longer abused alcohol or drugs, there had not been any return of depressive symptomatology, and she seemed to have a much more positive image of herself. She had not required any prescribed medication since the completion of the brief marital therapy. Mr. A. seemed much more in touch with himself and obviously was comfortable with his many affectionate messages to her.

This brief clinical vignette raises many questions, two of which seem directly relevant to our topic. The first is, has Mrs. A. changed? The second is, if so, what processes account for that change? I shall argue that Mrs. A. *has* really changed and that her change is a direct reflection of the change in her interpersonal context.

The issue of how change is measured is much debated. Perhaps the most generally accepted format involves the use of multiple indexes including, at the minimum, changes in behavior, changes in feelings about one's self, and, somewhat more controversially, changes in internal psychological structures. Mrs. A. no longer abuses alcohol or drugs and has had no recurrence of depressive symptoms. She is no longer anxious or belligerent and her feelings about herself are much more positive. The question of whether there have been changes in Mrs. A.'s internal psychological structures is unanswerable from the data at hand. Indeed, the issue of measurement of changes in internal psychological structures, particularly object representations, by something other than changes in transference projections has only recently begun to be explored.

Although I think that some colleagues would agree that the change in Mrs. A.'s behavior and affect, now sustained for four years, suggest that she has "really" changed, there is little likelihood of even that level of consensus about how such changes have occurred. Some observers would, I believe, suggest that the changes can best be understood as a transference cure, the introjective use of me by both partners. Others might focus on the degree to which I offered the couple mutually satisfactory interpretations, that the change is facilitated, in part, by insight. Still others might suggest that Mrs. A.'s changes have little, if anything, to do with the marital therapy. Rather, they represent her accommodation to a primitive transferential need to defeat powerful others, both her individual therapist and her husband. Although there may be some validity to such interpretations, they do not tell us as much as we need to know.

I would like to suggest that the changes in Mrs. A. have come about because of a substantial and enduring change in the marital relationship, a change which required the participation of both spouses. Further, on the basis of the work of a number of contemporary theorists, I wish to suggest plausible mechanisms with which to understand the changes in Mrs. A.

The question is the extent to which internal psychological structures are sustained or modified by ongoing interpersonal relationships. For heuristic purposes, let us assume that Mrs. A.'s fragile self-system was characterized by the unintegrated polarities of omnipotence-impotence and aggressor-victim. Further, that she often projected to Mr. A. the omnipotent and aggressor representations and experienced herself as the helpless victim. To what extent is Mr. A.'s behavioral acceptance of these projections essential to the maintenance of Mrs. A.'s internal psychological structures? How modifiable are those structures if, for internal reasons of his own, he stops both introjecting her projections and projecting to her his own impotent, victim object representations?

The issue of the extent to which the stabilization and continuance of internal psychological structures are dependent on interpersonal processes has a long and complex history that can be described only in part in this presentation. Doherty and Jacobson[8] have recently pointed out, for example, that among theoretical orientations only psychoanalysis and role theory emphasize that changes can occur in adult personality as a consequence of social interaction. Erickson's elaboration of the sociological dimensions of an evolving ego psychology,[9] Rapaport's concept of "stimulus nutrient,"[10, 11] and Hartman's focus on "social compliance"[12] are but a few of the earlier psychoanalytic contributions.

Benedek's work moved the focus to reciprocal processes in the normal parent-child relationship. She emphasizes that through introjections and identifications, internal structural changes occur in *both* child and parents.[13] Blanck and Blanck offer comparable insights into personality growth resulting from positive identifications within a marriage.[14]

A number of students of family systems observe similar or related phenomena; that is, relationships in which family members react to each other as if they were not themselves but someone very different. Vogel and Bell's concept of "scapegoating,"[15] Wynne's "trading of associations,"[16] and Bowen's "family projections processes"[17] are but examples from a long list of contributors. Ackerman early emphasized the need to understand that personality both unfolds autonomously from within and is influenced from without.[18]

This body of both psychoanalytic and family systems literature can be seen as the matrix from which a number of contemporary theorists have addressed the specific issue of the dependence of internal psychological structures on ongoing interpersonal relationships. I wish to focus selectively on a few recent contributors: Wachtel,[19] Zinner and Shapiro,[20] Ogden,[21, 22] and Meissner.[23]

Wachtel suggests that the role of interpersonal events in perpetuating neurosis is part of the common sense knowledge of most therapists but is not well integrated into the theories that guide their work. He emphasizes the cyclical recreation of interpersonal events and the real behavior of "accomplices" in perpetuating characterological patterns. Wishes, fantasies, and other internal structures must be understood as both independent and dependent variables. Wachtel specifically calls attention to the absence of a focus on such processes in the attempt to understand changes resulting from psychotherapy.

A concept central to the interaction between internal psychological structures and significant others is that of projective identification. Zinner and Shapiro describe the elements of that process as including the following: (1) The subject perceives the object as if the object contained elements of the subject's personality, (2) the subject can evoke object behavior that confirms the subject's perception, (3) the subject vicariously experiences the object's behavior and feelings, and (4) participants in close relationships often collude to sustain mutual projections. Depending on the content of the projected material, the subject's capacity to differentiate his or her self from the object, and the intensity of the subject's defensive requirements, the projective identification may result either in healthy, empathic qualities within the relationship or in attributions that bind the object to the subject's defensive economy.

Ogden describes projective identification as a psychological process that is simultaneously a type of defense, a mode of communication, a primitive form of object relationship, and a pathway for psychological change. He suggests that the process involves three phases: the unconscious fantasy of ridding oneself of an unwanted part of oneself by projecting that part into another person; the induction of congruent feelings in that person through a variety of interpersonal reactions; and the reinternalization of the processed projection by the projector. Under certain circumstances it is this last aspect of the projective identification that can lead to change in the internal structures of the projector. Ogden reviewed the contributions of those writers who point out the role of projective identification as one factor in effective psychotherapy for some, and particularly more primitive patients (Bion,[24, 25] Rosenfeld,[26, 27] Balint,[28, 29] Searles,[30, 31] Malin and Grotstein,[32] Kernberg,[33] Nadelson,[34] and Langs[35]).

Central to the perspective of this paper is the work of Meissner,[36] who, although specifically eschewing the use of the term projective identification, describes similar processes in formulating a transference model of marital interaction with a major focus on mutually interlocking projection-introjection systems. Less well differentiated individuals with fragile self-systems organized around the unintegrated polarities of inadequacy-hyperadequacy and victim-aggressor are drawn to each other. Each projects to the other object representations reflecting internalizations of conflicted, early relationships with parents, and the marital relationship can be understood as stabilized around such mutual projection-introjection mechanisms. Meissner emphasizes, however, that such mechanisms are but the foundation on which complex emergent qualities of the marital interaction are based. The marriage can't be totally understood by only understanding the projection-introjection systems. This transference model of marital interaction can help in understanding such processes as mellowing with age, the tendency of men to become more nurturing, of women to be more assertive with advancing age, and the increasing use of mature defences in George Valliant's better outcome subjects. It is suggested that one of the vehicles for adult personality development involves marital relationship.

Although Meissner emphasizes antecedent phenomena, that is, the levels of differentiation of the spouses as they enter the relationship, he recognizes the possibility of positive outcome, noting that the reactivation of older object relationships may allow for reworking – for therapeutic change or psychological growth. This point needs emphasis in order to begin to understand processes such as "mellowing with age," the tendency for men to become more nurturing and women more assertive with age,[37] and the increasing use of more mature defenses in Vaillant's better outcome subjects.[38]

To return to Mrs. A., I suggest that the brief marital therapy, made possible by a change in Mr. A.'s defensive economy, has resulted in significant change. Further, that the clear and sustained changes in her behavior and affect are accompanied by changes in her internal psychological structures brought about by alterations in Mr. and Mrs. A.'s interlocking projection-introjection systems. The point is that Mrs. A. has not just changed in affect and behavior and relationship to herself but those changes have been associated with internal changes. I suggest that the marital therapy played a role in what can be called a "recalibration" of a relationship. We were able, I believe, to seize an opportune moment and renegotiate one parameter of their relationship. This has led to a gradual change in their projection-introjection systems and, as a consequence, he has been able to experience himself as less powerful, more vulnerable; and she is less fixed in the self-experienced role of helpless victim.

It may be recalled, however, that the starting point for this chapter involved the influence of so-called outside factors on the effectiveness of individual psychotherapy. I would like to return to that perspective. In keeping with the concept that effective psychotherapy may result from different combinations of variables, clear and sustained changes in the individuals participating in successful marital or family therapy suggest the need for greater attention to marital and family variables in understanding effective individual psychotherapy. The results of individual psychotherapy may be decisively influenced in those patients whose symptomatology serves important, reciprocal needs of others in their entangled marital or family relationship. We need to recognize those circumstances that should alert us to that possibility. I will discuss only several of the more common clues.

The first circumstance involves the patient who enters the marital relationship in a clearly symptomatic state. Although there may be multiple reasons that account for the selection of a symptomatic partner, one possibility that should be entertained is that the patient's symptoms or level of maturation fulfill complementary needs in the spouse. This possibility is heightened in those marital relationships in which the partners organize their relation around stereotyped complementary roles: weak and strong, submissive and dominant, or victim and aggressor. A related issue is the failure of the relationship to have resulted in obvious change in each spouse, a failure in the healing function of marriage. Whether "marital healing" can occur below a certain level of personality organization is not known and will require sophisticated longitudinal studies of couples with varying levels of personality organization.

A second circumstance is that of the resistant spouse. In this situation the spouse, despite apparent concern about his or her partner, refuses to explore the ways in which he or she may be unconsciously participating in the partner's symptoms or behavior. Although once again there may be multiple reasons for such resistance, the possibility of interlocking projection-introjection systems should be entertained.

A third common circumstance is the spouse's defensive response to evidence that his or her partner has entered an early treatment alliance with the therapist or, more particularly, is beginning to project to the therapist internal object representations previously directed at the spouse. The defensive behavior of the spouse may involve overt anger towards the therapist or more subtle mechanisms. One possibility is that the spouse is reacting to the early manifestations of an emerging instability in the previously rigid interlocking projection-introjection systems. A related circumstance is that in which clinical improvement in the patient is followed closely by the development of a symptomatic state in the spouse. Here the presumption is that the therapist has replaced to some degree the spouse as the recipient of the patient's transference projections with a resulting change in the spouse's defensive economy and the development of symptoms. Another related circumstance is the spouse who begins for the first time to raise the possibility of divorce following the patient's early improvement.

These clinical situations are common to many of us. What is perhaps somewhat less obvious is the need to consider the presence of interlocking projection-introjection systems within the marriages or families of patients who are unusually resistant, difficult to engage in treatment alliances, or who appear ready to break off the therapeutic encounter almost before it begins. For some patients the resistance to treatment may be both intrapsychic and within the marital or family system.

In our continuing efforts to understand the factors that account for successful individual psychotherapy, I suggest that increased clinical sensitivity to the role of marital and family factors will be helpful. The designs of future psychotherapy research studies should involve methods of controlling for or measuring the impact of marital and family factors on the effectiveness of individual psychotherapy. These, I believe, are two important steps by which together we can persist in the effort both to understand better those processes that are crucial for healing and to find increased social support for those psychotherapies that many of us believe are the most powerful agents of human change yet devised.

NOTES

1. Frank, J. D. The present status of outcome studies. *J Consult Clin Psychol*, 1979, *47*(2), 310-316.

2. American Psychiatric Association Commission on Psychotherapies, *Psychotherapy Research: Methodological and Efficacy Issues*. Washington, D.C.: American Psychiatric Association, 1982.

3. Leff, J. P., and Vaughn, C. E. The interaction of life events and relatives' expressed emotion in schizophrenia and depressive neurosis. *Br J Psychiatry*, 1980, *136*, 146-153.

4. Vaughn, C. E., and Leff, J. P. The influence of family and social factors on the course of psychiatric illness. *Br J Psychiatry*, 1976, *129*, 125-137.

5. Vaughn, C. E., Snyder, K. S., Freeman, W., Jones, S., Falloon, I. R. H., and Liberman, R. P. Family factors in schizophrenic relapse: A replication. *Schizophr Bull*, 1982, *8*(2), 425-426.

6. Lewis, J. M. Dying with friends: Implications for the psychotherapist. *Am J Psychiatry*, March, 1982, 261-266.

7. Lewis, J. M. The inward eye: Monitoring the process of psychotherapy. *Journal of Continuing Education in Psychiatry*, July, 1979, 17-26.

8. Doherty, W. J., and Jacobson, N. S. Marriage and the family. In B. B. Wolman (Ed.), *Handbook of Developmental Psychology*. Englewood Cliffs, N.J.: Prentice-Hall, 1982, 667-680.

9. Erickson, E. H. *Childhood and Society*. New York: Norton, 1950.

10. Rapaport, D. The theory of ego autonomy: A generalization. *Bull Menninger Clin*, 1958, *22*, 13-35.

11. Rapaport, D. On the psychoanalytic theory of motivation. In N. M. Gill (Ed.), *The Collected Papers of David Rapaport*. New York: Basic Books, 1967, 853-915.

12. Hartmann, H. Psychoanalysis and sociology. In H. Hartmann *Essays on Ego Psychology*. New York: International Universities Press, 1964.

13. Benedek, T. Parenthood as a developmental phase. *J Psychoanal Assoc*, 1957, *7*, 389-417.

14. Blanck, W., and Blanck, G. *Marriage and Personal Development*. New York: Columbia University Press, 1968.

15. Vogel, E. F., and Bell, N. W. The emotionally disturbed child as the family scapegoat. In N. W. Bell and E. F. Vogel (Eds.), *A Modern Introduction to the Family*. Glencoe: The Free Press, 1980.

16. Wynne, L. C. Some indications and contraindications for exploratory family therapy. In I. Boszormenyi-Nagy and J. L. Framo (Eds.), *Intensive Family Therapy*. New York: Hoeber, 1965, 289-322.

17. Bowen, M. Family psychotherapy with schizophrenia in the hospital and in private practice. In I. Boszormenyi-Nagy, and J. L. Framo (Eds.), *Intensive Family Therapy*. New York: Hoeber, 1965.

18. Ackerman, N. W. *The Psychodynamics of Family Life*. New York: Basic Books, 1958.

19. Wachtel, P. L. *Psychoanalysis and Behavior Therapy*. New York: Basic Books, 1977.

20. Zinner, J., and Shapiro, R. Projective identification as a mode of perception and behaviour in families of adolescents. *Int J Psychoanal*, 1972, *53*, 523-530.

21. Ogden, T. H. On projective identification. *Int J Psychoanal*, 1979, *60*, 357-373.

22. Ogden, T. H. Projective identification in psychiatric hospital treatment. *Bull Menninger Clin*, 1981, *45*(4), 317-333.

23. Meissner, W. W. The conceptualization of marriage and family dynamics from a psychoanalytic perspective. In T. J. Paolino, Jr., and B. S. McCrady (Eds.), *Marriage and Marital Therapy*. New York: Brunner/Mazel, 1978.

24. Bion, W. *Experiences in Groups*. New York: Basic Books, 1959.

25. Bion, W. Attacks on linking. *Int J Psychoanal*, 1959, *40*, 308-315.

26. Rosenfeld, H. Transference phenomena and transference analysis in an acute catatonic schizophrenic patient. *Int J Psychoanal*, 1952, *33*, 457-464.

27. Rosenfeld, H. Considerations regarding the psychoanalytic approach to acute and chronic schizophrenia. *Int J Psychoanal*, 1954, *35*, 135-140.

28. Balint, M. *Primary Love and Psychoanalytic Technique*. New York: Liveright Publishing Co., 1965.

29. Balint, M. *The Basic Fault*. London: Tavistock, 1968.

30. Searles, H. Transference psychosis in the psychotherapy of schizophrenia. In *Collected Papers on Schizophrenia and Related Subjects*. New York: International Universities Press, 1965.

31. Searles, H. The patient as therapist to the analyst. In P. Giovacchini (Ed.), *Tactics and Techniques in Psychoanalytic Psychotherapy, Vol. 2*. New York: Jason Aronson, 1975.

32. Malin, A., and Grotstein, J. Projective identification in the therapeutic process. *Int J Psychoanal*, 1966, *47*, 26-31.

33. Kernberg, O. Normal and pathological development. In *Object Relations Theory and Clinical Psychoanalysis*. New York: Jason Aronson, 1976.

34. Nadelson, T. Victim, victimizer: Interaction in the psychotherapy of borderline patients. *Int J Psychoanal*, 1976, *5*, 115-129.

35. Langs, R. *The Therapeutic Interaction*. New York: Jason Aronson, 1976.

36. Meissner, W. W. The schizophrenic and the paranoid process. *Schizophr Bull*, 1981, *7*(4), 611-631.

37. Neugarten, B. L., and Guttman, D. L. Age, sex roles and personality in middle age: A thematic apperception study. In B. L. Neugarten (Ed.), *Middle Age and Aging*. Chicago: University of Chicago Press, 1968, 58.

38. Vaillant, G. E. *Adaptation to Life*. Boston: Little, Brown, & Company, 1977.

2

Therapeutic Components of All Psychotherapies

Jerome D. Frank

    The distinguishing feature of the kinds of distress and disability for which psychotherapy is believed to be the treatment of choice is that they create perturbations in the patient's communications with others. These disturbed communications, which, for want of a better term, I shall call psychiatric symptoms, concern distressing subjective states arising from a maladaptive "assumptive world," that is, the structure and content of the patient's assumptions about himself, his future and the world about him (Frank, 1973). In turn, these assumptions lead to behavior that produces distress in the patient, and usually in others as well.

    To the extent that cure is viewed as the eradication of the causes of an illness, a few words about the causes of psychiatric illnesses are in order. Since humans are open systems in which psychological and biological components as well as aspects of the environment interact, these causes can lie anywhere in the system. They can be in the body, primarily but not necessarily exclusively in the central nervous system; in destructive early life experiences; or in current stressful interactions with others.

The only features of psychiatric symptoms directly modifiable by psychotherapy are their functions or meanings. These are determined by stressful aspects of the patient's assumptive world. The form of the symptoms, such as hallucinations, anxiety attacks, or obsessions, is probably determined by properties of the central nervous system.

For example, a kindergarten teacher was beset by a recurrent obsession that she had run over a child in returning from work, and plagued her husband for reassurance that she had not done so. The meaning or function of this symptom could plausibly be accounted for by certain life experiences that had shaped her assumptive world. Her parents had always favored an emotionally fragile younger sister and criticized the patient for her bad temper, which she came to regard as a serious personal flaw. The symptom appeared shortly after her marriage to a man whom she felt neglected her because of preoccupation with his work. She could not openly express her resentment because, she claimed, he had told her that a wife should never be angry at her husband. Her symptoms could easily be interpreted as expressions of anger at her sister deflected onto school children, as well as oblique ways of simultaneously eliciting attention from her husband and expressing her anger at him. That is, given the neurotic symptom, one can always find a plausible psychodynamic explanation for it. The reverse, however, does not hold — given a psychodynamic formulation, one cannot predict the form of the symptom. With the same upbringing and marriage, the patient might equally well have developed hysterical fits, or agoraphobia, or compulsive checking of the automobile brake, to name a few possibilities. Whatever the particular form of the symptom, it would have the same psychodynamically determined meaning, however, as part of the patient's way of adjusting to her current life situation.

Turning now to the crucial words in the title of this symposium, "psychotherapy" and "cures," a definition of psychotherapy that encompasses the wide range of activities for which this term is used, while at the same time excluding helpful activities by relatives, friends or casual acquaintances like bartenders, would be: psychotherapy is a confiding, emotionally charged relationship between a trained, socially sanctioned healer and a sufferer. The healer seeks to relieve the patient's suffering and disability, which both assume to be primarily of psychological origin, by a procedure, often involving other patients or family members, that is organized in terms of a particular conceptual scheme. Psychotherapy is conducted by means of symbolic communications — primarily words but, in some methods, also activities with symbolic components as in bioenergetics (Lowen, 1975).

As to "cures," if by this term, eradication of the causes of an illness is meant, features of the patient's illness that psychotherapy can cure directly would be those caused by stress-producing distortions in the patient's assumptive world. Since the patient is an open psychobiological system, correction of these distortions would inevitably be reflected in changes in the neurophysiology of the central nervous system.

The amenability of psychiatric symptoms to psychotherapy, then, depends on the accessibility of their "organic" component to symbolic inputs. Accessibility seems to differ with the nature of the psychological manifestations; thus the neurological substrates of anxiety seem more modifiable by psychotherapy than the neurological correlates of obsessions.

By changing the meaning or function of a symptom for a patient, psychotherapy may cause it to diminish, or even vanish, without affecting the tendency of the nervous system to react in a similar way should stresses be renewed. Thus the patient with obsessions became almost symptom-free after she learned how to express her anger at her husband directly and he responded appropriately by paying more attention to her. Some three years after the end of treatment, however, in the setting of a strange city where her husband was preoccupied with the demands of a new job and she had to cope with two babies and the presence of her ill sister, the patient's obsessions recurred, though not in as severe a form.

With luck, changes in the assumptive world produced by psychotherapy can result in changes in thinking and behavior that yield more satisfactions and are thereby reinforced, creating a benevolent circle so that the patient continues to hold or increase the gains achieved by therapy.

Actually, cure is usually too ambitious a term to apply to the results of most psychotherapeutic procedures with most patients. More typically the goal of psychotherapy is improvement, and it is closer to rehabilitation medicine than to curative medicine, that is, psychotherapy seeks to help the patient alter his or her assumptive world in such a way that the patient becomes better able to utilize potentialities and to circumvent or minimize liabilities.

To descend from the theoretical to the empirical, the evidence is overwhelming that all forms of psychotherapy produce greater effect size than no treatment over the same period of time. If this were not the case, psychotherapy broadly defined would not have persisted over millennia as an important social institution. Its general helpfulness has been repeatedly confirmed by two types of research. The first consists of individual studies, of which the study of Sloane et al., (1975) comparing behavior therapy and analytically-oriented therapy, is a landmark. The relative superiority of psychotherapy of whatever form over no-treatment control groups has also been conclusively demonstrated by massive meta-analyses of controlled studies of psychotherapy by Smith, Glass and Miller (1980) and Shapiro and Shapiro (1982).

Comparison of one form of therapy with another, however, has failed to demonstrate convincingly that any one is superior to any of the others for most psychiatric illnesses. Possible exceptions to this conclusion are that, for example, cognitive therapy may be superior for depressed outpatients (Rush et al, 1977) and that behavior therapy may be suitable for a wider range of patients than analytically oriented therapies (Sloane et al, 1975). In any case, schools of psychotherapy proliferate and endure, which can only mean that each is helpful to some patients. This is also supported by the studies just mentioned. None of them found either behavior therapy or interview therapy for unselected outpatients to be clearly more efficacious than the other.

In passing, it must be emphasized that the failure to find differences in effectiveness of different forms of psychotherapy does not mean that such differences do not exist. Despite the many methodological weaknesses in the studies surveyed, however (Parloff, 1980), at the very least their findings suggest that therapeutic features shared by all forms of psychotherapy account for a considerable portion of their effectiveness.

This conclusion seems to conflict with widespread clinical experience of most psychotherapists, each of whom has been able to help patients greatly who have failed with other therapists or other forms of therapy. The purpose of the remainder of this presentation is to suggest and offer support for a hypothesis that is consistent with both experimental findings and clinical impressions.

This hypothesis is that most patients come to psychotherapy, not because of specific symptoms alone, but because the symptoms have demoralized them, and that features shared by all forms of psychotherapy and which account for much of their effectiveness combat this demoralization (Frank, 1974; de Figueiredo & Frank 1982).

Demoralization may be defined as a state of subjective incapacity plus distress. The patient suffers from a sense of failure, loss of self-esteem, feelings of hopelessness or helplessness and feelings of alienation or isolation. These are often accompanied by a sense of mental confusion which the patient may express as a fear of insanity.

The most common symptoms of psychiatric outpatients — and the symptoms most responsive to any form of psychotherapy — are anxiety and depression (Sloane et al., 1975; Smith, Glass and Miller, 1980). These can be viewed as direct expressions of demoralization. Other symptoms, whatever their cause, interact with demoralization in two ways. First, they increase it by decreasing the patient's coping capacity, and, secondly, they wax and wane with the extent of demoralization, so that reducing the demoralization can ameliorate the symptoms. Thus the patient mentioned earlier, when asked at a three-year follow-up point what had helped her most, stated "You made me feel like a real person." Similarly, some patients with panic attacks improve considerably if they can be convinced that the attacks are not dangerous and are always transient (Weeks, 1977); that is, although they may still have panic attacks, these no longer cause as much distress or interfere significantly with their living patterns. Even schizophrenic symptoms may be diminished by the restoration of a patient's morale. One woman, for example, phoned me during Christmas vacation because she was a visitor in my city and had been given my name. She stated that she was schizophrenic, that she was on Stelazine, but that she was beginning to hallucinate and to giggle and was afraid that she was about to suffer a relapse. I was able briefly to reassure her on the phone. Six weeks later she wrote that "After receiving your opinion that my regular dose of Stelazine would probably control my symptoms I returned to good functioning again. Just to be reassured by a competent psychiatrist that I and Stelazine are in control of the situation is the best therapy possible for me!"

Features common to all therapy that combat demoralization are stimulation of hope and enhancement of the patient's sense of mastery over his own feelings and environmental challenges. The therapist fosters these attitudes by procedures which, guided by a coherent conceptual scheme, strengthen the therapeutic relationship, provide new information, especially of the experiential type, and enable the patient to organize and make sense out of hitherto inexplicable experiences.

This view of therapy is supported by evidence from several sources. Surveys from various populations comparing those who have been or are in psychotherapy with those who have never had psychotherapy consistently reveal that the former had a higher incidence or greater severity of social isolation, helplessness or sense of failure (Frank, 1982). Surveys of populations using a variety of scales of psychopathology revealed that eight were so highly correlated that they must have been measuring the same thing. These were essentially those listed above as symptoms of demoralization. Using these scales, it was found that about four-fifths of patients clinically impaired were also demoralized (Dohrenwend et al., 1980; Dohrenwend and Crandall, 1970).

Further support comes from the repeated observation that patients seek psychotherapy only after their symptoms have persisted for quite a while and other forms of help have failed. The average time lapse between the first symptoms of alcoholism and seeking medical help is five years (Mandell, 1983); for those with chronic panic states, twelve years (Shader, Goodman and Gever, 1982); and in an ordinary outpatient clinic, six months to two years (Karasu, 1982) — that is, patients do not seek help until their symptoms have demoralized them.

Also consistent with the demoralization hypothesis is the common observation that the "good" patient is someone who is distressed but has good ego-strength and is able to utilize helping relationships (Strupp, 1976) — that is, he is motivated to undergo therapy and has personal qualities that enable him to profit from it.

Turning to the therapist, the evidence is persuasive that personal characteristics of the therapist in interaction with those of the patient are more important than technique in determining the outcome of treatment. In one study, for example, the most successful patient-therapist combinations yielded a 100 percent improvement rate, while the worst yielded one-third improved, one-third the same, and one-third worse (Orlinsky and Howard, 1980).

The findings of a study of encounter groups are also relevant. Although not offered as therapy, many of these groups use some procedures of therapy groups and are sought by persons also in psychotherapy (Lieberman, 1977). The study included two leaders from each of several schools. In one such pair using the same method, one leader obtained the best results and one the worst of the entire study (Lieberman, Yalom and Miles, 1973).

These findings are consistent with the general impression that among practitioners of each technique, some are more successful than others because of certain still indefinable personal qualities. These seem to be related to the therapist's ability to convey to the patient that he or she takes him seriously, understands him and is able to inspire the patient's hopes for improvement. Some therapists seem able to communicate these and other therapeutic attitudes to most of their patients. Others are less fortunate, but, as mentioned earlier, all of us have succeeded with some patients with whom other therapists have failed. In short, while procedures may be largely interchangeable in determining outcome, therapists are not.

With respect to the procedures themselves, a finding consistent with the demoralization hypothesis is that many patients benefit greatly from a single interview, that is, before the therapist's specific technique can play a part (Wells, 1982). The average number of clinic interviews is only five or six (Garfield, 1980). Of course, many patients drop out of therapy early because therapy has failed them, but this explanation could not account for all early terminators. For example, in a study of ours, those patients who dropped out after less than four sessions showed significant symptom relief, although not as marked as those who had been in treatment four to six months (Frank, 1978). Along the same lines, patients who were placed on a waiting list after a three-hour intake interview with a psychiatrist showed a 70 percent improvement rate, suggesting that they experienced the assessment interview as therapeutic (Sloane et al., 1975). This would explain a similar finding of our own early work in which patients showed a marked drop in discomfort after receiving a battery of tests and interviews which the researchers perceived as diagnostic and the patients as therapeutic (Frank, 1978).

Perhaps the most striking evidence that many of the beneficial effects of psychotherapy result from its ability to combat demoralization is that symptom relief produced by psychotherapy is the same on the average as that produced by placebo. We found this in our work, and it has recently been confirmed by a study using a subset of the studies analyzed by Smith, Glass and Miller (1980), in which the effects of psychotherapy were compared with those of a "placebo treatment," this being defined as any procedure that lacks the specific features of the therapy with which it is being compared (Prioleau et al., 1983).

The proper interpretation of these findings, I believe, is that the placebo procedures contain the ingredients of psychotherapy that are necessary and sufficient for combatting demoralization, namely a helping person who listens to the patient's complaints and then offers a procedure the patient believes will relieve them, thereby inspiring the patient's hopes.

The demoralization hypothesis is consistent, not only with the general failure to find significant differences in effect size for different therapies, but also with the slight difference in favor of cognitive and behavioral therapies found in some studies (Sloane et al., 1975; Shapiro and Shapiro, 1982). Most patients come to therapy for relief of more or less specific symptoms or problems in living. Cognitive and behavioral methods, by focusing on these, would therefore more closely conform to the expectations of many patients than unfocused, open-ended approaches. Furthermore, practitioners of cognitive and behavioral therapies interact continually with their patients and maintain an encouraging, hopeful attitude, thus providing a strong, morale-enhancing relationship.

It may well be that the success of a therapist with particular patients depends on how consonant the therapeutic program is with the patient's style of problem solving. For example, interview therapies might be most successful with patients who are introspective and self-analytical; behavioral therapies and cognitive therapies would be especially attractive to patients who actively try to solve problems, either by actions or rational thinking; and humanistic therapies might appeal most to the philosophically-minded.

A personal characteristic that may prove to be highly associated with differences in the success of therapeutic approaches with different patients is locus of control (Rotter, 1966). We found that patients with an internal locus of control benefited more from a therapy in which improvement was attributed to the patient's own efforts than from one in which improvement was attributed to a placebo pill, while patients with an external locus of control showed a reverse response (Liberman, 1978).

So much for the clinical and experimental evidence that for those patients whose symptoms seem to respond equally well to a wide range of psychotherapies the healing ingredient of these therapies is the ability of the therapist and the procedure to inspire the patient's hopes and increase self-confidence. What about the patients who are therapeutic failures in these studies? The Dohrenwends found that certain symptoms are not correlated with demoralization, and these turn out to be symptoms or behavioral manifestations that are unusually refractory to psychotherapy. These include false beliefs and perceptions, insomnia, passive-aggressive behavior, anti-social history, approval of rule-breaking, active expression of hostility, sex problems, distrust, rigidity and problems due to drinking (Dohrenwend et al., 1980). Some of these sources of distress and disability respond to medications. In any case, it seems reasonable to assume that, whatever their central nervous system correlates, these are more resistant to the morale-lifting components of psychotherapy than complaints primarily expressive of demoralization. If any psychotherapies can significantly affect them, they would have to be sufficiently powerful to influence the underlying neuropathology.

Possible evidence of such power would be that they produce very strong emotional reactions or altered states of consciousness.

Perhaps not surprisingly, it turns out that these very therapies are systematically excluded from the surveys of therapies already mentioned. This is not hard to understand. Their practitioners are usually messianic characters like Janov (1970) or — if one considers cults to be forms of psychotherapy — Werner Erhart (Rhinehart, 1976), and many others, who have no real interest in testing the validity of their claims through controlled experiments. At the same time, these emotionally charged, highly dramatic procedures are not congenial to the temperament of researchers. Therefore, it remains possible that patients found to be unimproved in the surveys cited might have responded favorably to some of the excluded therapeutic approaches.

In this connection, the power of these to lift morale is very strong. They inspire hope through the highly dramatic nature of the proceedings, as well as through the mobilization of strong group expectations and support. Persons who come through them unscathed, furthermore, are certain to experience an increase in self-confidence by virtue of the very fact that they found themselves able to withstand intense emotional upheavals.

Whether among these therapies certain procedures would be more beneficial for some conditions than others remains an open question in the absence of data.

To sum up, at least 75 percent of all outpatients seeking psychotherapy, whatever their presenting symptoms, are also demoralized. This condition is potentially curable by features shared by all forms of psychotherapy: a therapeutic relationship in which the therapist demonstrates concern for the patient and provides a rationale and a procedure related to it. The relationship, rationale, and procedure combat demoralization by increasing the patient's hopes and feelings of self-confidence through providing success experiences and enabling the patient to make sense out of distressing subjective states. As a result, if all goes well, the patient becomes able to cope more successfully with the stresses that brought him into therapy, leading to progressive improvement.

By alleviating demoralization, all forms of psychotherapy cure symptoms such as certain types of anxiety and depression that directly express this state of mind, and other symptoms that are aggravated by demoralization may be relieved, as well. Differences in effectiveness of psychotherapy depend more on the morale-enhancing features of different patient-therapist pairs than on differences in procedures.

The responsiveness of demoralization to psychotherapy suggests that, whatever neuropathological processes underlie it, they are modifiable by psychological inputs. Neuropathological processes underlying symptoms less closely related to demoralization seem more resistant to psychological influences. Whether any form of psychotherapy can do more than alleviate the demoralization accompanying these symptoms is an open question. Perhaps therapies which produce markedly altered states of consciousness or strong emotional upheavals, suggesting that their impact on the central nervous system is powerful, can directly ameliorate these symptoms, but this remains to be determined.

NOTES

deFigueiredo, J. M., and Frank, J. D. Subjective incompetence, the clinical hallmark of demoralization. *Compr Psychiatry*, 1982, *23*, 353-363.

Dohrenwend, B. P., and Crandall, D. L. Psychiatric symptoms in community, clinic and mental hospital groups. *Am J Psychiatry*, 1970, *126*, 1611-1621.

Dohrenwend, B. P., Shrout, P. E., Egri, G., and Mendelsohn, F. S. Nonspecific psychological distress and other dimensions of psychopathology, measures for use in the general population. *Arch Gen Psychiatry*, 1980, *37*, 1229-1236.

Frank, J. D. *Persuasion and Healing* (2d. ed.). Baltimore: Johns Hopkins University Press, 1973.

Frank, J. D. Psychotherapy: The restoration of morale. *Am J Psychiatry*, 1974, *131*, 271-274.

Frank, J. D. Expectation and therapeutic outcome — the placebo effect and the role induction interview. In J. D. Frank, R. Hoehn-Saric, S. D. Imber, B. L. Liberman, and A. R. Stone, *Effective Ingredients of Successful Psychotherapy*. New York: Brunner/Mazel, 1978.

Frank, J. D. Therapeutic components shared by all psychotherapies. In J. H. Harvey and M. M. Parks (Eds.), *Psychotherapy Research and Behavior Change* (The Master Lecture Series, Vol. 1). Washington, D.C.: American Psychological Association, 1982.

Garfield, S. Psychotherapy: *An Eclectic Approach*. New York: John Wiley & Sons, 1980.

Janov, A. *The Primal Scream*. New York: Putnam, 1970.

Karasu, B. Personal communication, 1982.

Liberman, B. L. The role of mastery in psychotherapy: Maintenance of improvement and prescriptive change. In J. D. Frank, R. Hoehn-Saric, S. D. Imber, B. L. Liberman, and A. R. Stone, *Effective Ingredients of Successful Psychotherapy*. New York: Brunner/Mazel, 1978.

Lieberman, M. A. Problems in integrating traditional group therapies with new forms. *Int J Group Psychother*, 1977, *27*, 19-32.

Lieberman, M. A., Yalom, I. D., and Miles, M. B. *Encounter Groups: First Facts*. New York: Basic Books, 1973.

Lowen, A. *Bioenergetics*. New York: Coward, McCann & Geoghegan, 1975.

Mandell, W. Types and phases of alcohol dependence. In M. Galanter (Ed.), *Recent Developments in Alcoholism*. New York: Plenum, 1983.

Orlinsky, D. E., and Howard, K. I. Gender and psychotherapeutic outcome. In A. Brodsky and R. T. Hare-Mustin (Eds.), *Women and Psychotherapy*. New York: Guilford Press, 1980.

Parloff, M. B. Psychotherapy research: An anaclitic depression. *Psychiatry*, 1980, *43*, 279-293.

Prioleau, L., Murdock, M., and Brody, N. An analysis of psychotherapy vs. acebo studies. *The Behavioral & Brain Sciences*, 1983, *6*, 275-310.

Rhinehart, L. *The Book of est*. New York: Holt, Rinehart & Winston, 1976.

Rotter, J. B. Generalized expectancies for internal vs. external control of reinforcement. *Psychological Monographs*, 1966, *80*, No. 1 (whole No. 609).

Rush, A. J., Beck, A. T., Kovacs, M., and Hollon, S. Comparative effects of cognitive therapy and pharmacotherapy in the treatment of depressed outpatients. *Cognitive Therapy & Research*, 1977, *1*, 17-37.

Shader, R. I., Goodman, M., and Gever, J. Panic disorders: Current perspectives. *Journal of Clinical Psychopharmacology*, 1982, *2*, No. 6 (Suppl.), 25-105.

Shapiro, D. A., and Shapiro, D. Meta-analysis of comparative therapy outcome studies: A replication and refinement. *Psychol Bull*, 1982, *92*, 581-604.

Sloane, R. B., Staples, F. R., Cristol, A. H., Yorkston, N. J., and Whipple, K. *Psychotherapy Versus Behavior Therapy*. Cambridge, Mass.: Harvard University Press, 1975.

Smith, N. L., Glass, G. V., and Miller, T. I. *Benefits of Psychotherapy*. Baltimore: Johns Hopkins University Press, 1980.

Strupp, H. The nature of the therapeutic influence and its basic ingredients. In A. Burton (Ed.), *What Makes Behavior Change Possible*. New York: Brunner/Mazel, 1976.

Weeks, C. *Agoraphobia*. New York: Dutton, 1977.

Wells, R. A. *Planned Short-term Treatment*. New York: The Free Press, 1982.

3

Finding the Issues: Dialogue I

DR. ROBERT MICHELS (Moderator): Dr. Lewis and Dr. Frank find that wide array of processes occur in psychotherapy and select a different few to focus upon. Dr. Lewis tells us that behavior is maintained by the patient's social network and that changes in that social network may be the essential contributors to change in the individual. He gives a vivid case example where the intervention was directly in the social network and then speculates that the impact of individual therapy on the social network may be an important intervening variable in its potential efficacy as an agent of change. Dr. Frank reminds us of his classic contribution to the understanding of what it is that psychotherapy may be about in the first place: that whatever the primary disorder, there is a near universal secondary

disorder of demoralization, and it is the efficacy of the human therapeutic relationship on the secondary disorder that may be the major
or sole mechanism of action in psychotherapy. He points out the
immense power of the treatment of demoralization.

I think Dr. Frank is often misread. I think he is often read
as being a therapeutic nihilist, but I, at least, read him as being a
therapeutic optimist recognizing the immense power of this single
mode of action. He goes on uncharacteristically to me, to speculate
that in spite of this there may be specific modes of action in psychotherapy focusing more on nondisorder characteristics of the patient.
He cites examples such as cognitive style characteristics, or psychological attributes that may not be associated with the disorder being
treated but may be critical variables in determining what aspects of
the therapist, or perhaps even the therapy, might be most effective
for that patient. He points to the statistical difficulty of identifying
an effective therapy when we don't know what the critical variables
are, when we may be working with therapies which are differentially
effective only for very small subsets of the total being treated, and
when the noise will obscure the message unless we learn, before
doing the research, how to tune the receiver more sharply.

So we have on the table the question of specificity versus
non-specificity in psychotherapy. We have on the table the question of intrapsychic versus interpersonal interviewing mechanisms.
Dr. Frank takes the more classical position: Psychotherapy does
something to the patient's mind. In fact, he argues that's all it can
do. Dr. Lewis' suggestion is that psychotherapy does something
to the person's mind, but what it does to the person's mind changes
the person's relationships so that we then see a secondary stable
change in the person's personality. Those are not incompatible but
rather different points of view, and Drs. Lewis and Frank are emphasizing different aspects of this particular elephant.

What I'm going to do is ask each of the four other faculty to
comment on, and respond to, the two papers that we've heard, and
then, perhaps, have some interaction among the six. Finally we will
give Drs. Lewis and Frank a chance for some final comments. Dr.
Ornstein, I'm confident, will have some objections to some of what
we've heard so I'm going to start with him.

DR. PAUL ORNSTEIN: Let me start with just a very general comment first and then turn to some of the issues in both papers. I recognize the value of calling everything one human being, called "therapist," does with another human being, called "patient," psychotherapy. This allows us to view all healing efforts throughout the ages as forms of psychotherapy, at least in terms of their impact and outcome on the problem treated. Beyond this general advantage, however, I see no further advantages to lumping everything we do, in relation to people who come to us with distress, as psychotherapy. Now, here I have another problem that I will explicate later. I also differentiate between this general form of treatment, called psychotherapy, and the treatment called psychoanalytic psychotherapy, which I will also explicate later. What makes modern psychoanalytic psychotherapy, then, different from just psychotherapy? What are their common elements? And how can I, on the basis of this distinction, take a stance in relation to both Dr. Lewis' exposition, which I found very lucid and compelling in many ways, and also, of course, Dr. Frank's with whose ideas I've been more familiar for quite some time, as a matter of fact since my residency training?

Dr. Lewis, I think, made the courageous statement that in relation to Mr. & Mrs. A., the change is real change. Well what is real change in contrast to *not* real change? The psychoanalytic notion of an intrapsychic structural change is such a complex issue that I only want to comment on the fact that perhaps real change means that something within the patient, irrespective of the impact of the environment, remains or becomes solidly different and stays that way. However, I also believe that the change that takes place in a relationship, a marital relationship, is also real change, but of a different sort. What is the difference? If intrapsychic change means that somehow, as a result of the treatment process, new structures have to be built, or to put it differently, a developmental step that had not been taken before now is belatedly completed, then, of course, that is the real intrapsychic change. On the other hand, if that internal step or that belated developmental step is not taken but the relationship of the couple changes, that is also, I think, a real change that can for a very very long time sustain a new equilibrium and thereby, I think, can be considered a form of good, admirable, psychotherapeutic result.

In the case of this couple, over a four year period something was sustained; so I would accept the notion that real change may have occurred. But I feel we need to make the distinction. Dr. Lewis made it very clear that he was talking about outside factors. Later perhaps we can discuss what is outside and what is inside. That may shed some additional light on this. For the moment I would only like to say that I have certain questions about the manner in which that change of equilibrium was established between this couple, but that is again something that would lead more to emphasizing the differences.

I'm more impressed by the similarities and the bridges that can be built to these first two contributions, so I will stress them now and perhaps later on join the controversy. I find Dr. Frank's term, *demoralization*, as the central issue of the treatment process, as we look upon it from the broad perspective which he presented, a rather felicitous one. Although in my own thinking I would translate that term, or retranslate it, into something different, I find it very congenial because he has left mental apparatus psychology behind and he has embraced a personal psychology, or in my terms, a self-psychology. Demoralization, in my vocabulary, means that we are confronted with a self in a state of enfeeblement or fragmentation who turns for help to a psychotherapist. Everything he describes as the ingredients of the therapeutic process I can see, in my terminology, as a strengthening of that self structure, a reestablishment of the cohesiveness of the self, its vigor and vitality, which, when that happens, takes care of the so-called specific and, in Dr. Michels' terms, the primary symptoms. I think Dr. Michels, in rephrasing what Dr. Frank said, called something else primary and demoralization secondary. I would call demoralization equally primary and what Dr. Michels pictures as primary just a manifestation of that demoralization. In other words, symptomatology is secondary to the enfeeblement and fragmentation of the self. So if you can deal with the patient, and by whatever means reestablish that moral fiber so he doesn't feel demoralized, then, of course, you have helped him. Sometimes that can be done on the basis of those general approaches that Dr. Frank emphasizes. Other times, the specific issues that emerge once a demoralization occurred also have to be included.

DR. ROBERT MICHELS: Dr. Ornstein alerts us to the distinction that we're going to hear over and over again between real therapy and nice helping maneuvers that people do with patients using a theory other than "my own," which are often felicitous and helpful. The verb I think conjugates "I psychoanalyze, you do therapy, and they counsel," or something like that. We see some of this in the suggestion that Dr. Lewis alerted us to in his paper. Some will see this change as a transference cure, either in response to Dr. Lewis or in the acting out of a negative transference toward the previous therapist. But Dr. Lewis argues in the paper that there is more than that here. There is something going on that is stable and internal. Dr. Ornstein alerts us to something which I suspect we will hear from him later, in more detail – that before we call a change stable and internal we have to see evidence for a developmental process that was arrested, and that the treatment was allowed to resume and to fulfill a potential that had not previously been fulfilled. In the absence of that developmental process Dr. Ornstein says there isn't a real change, but only a phenotypic change; that is an issue Dr. Lewis has not, I think in the paper at least, explicitly addressed. As to whether demoralization is primary or secondary, Dr. Frank has to speak for himself. I think Dr. Frank sees demoralization as coming out of the meaning the patient places upon something, but there is a something there that Dr. Frank, I believe, locates in the nervous system, and I think Dr. Ornstein feels is probably a mix of categories that he's a little uncomfortable with.

DR. LEON SALZMAN: I find both felicitous and very congenial the presentations from Dr. Frank and Dr. Lewis. Precisely these issues, which Dr. Michels clarified so well, are the ones we must come to and deal with. What is real? What is unreal? And what is deep and what is superficial? Whether psychotherapy is only a stepchild of the magnificent parent called psychoanalysis, and so forth. What Dr. Lewis so amply, and I think supportively, presented to us was that change (which is our profession, if we presume to be able to intervene and overcome disturbed living) has to be manifest to the world at large, not only inside that person. It simply is not enough to talk about how well the patient understands himself unless this is translated into living. Now living means some productive exchange with some creative activity. It doesn't have to be with a person, but it has to be manifest, and it has to be visible, and it has to be understandable through some observational technique. I think we've had presentations from Dr. Lewis and Dr. Frank, which talk about manifest behavioral characteristics — issues that we can examine, report on, get some consensus about and, hopefully, build a science of behavior on. The other alternative, somehow, is too bogged down in very heavy mechanical constructs that perhaps are not so clearly visible, and I think Dr. Ornstein will speak heavily from that framework.

I was particularly interested in this concept of demoralization and the case which Dr. Frank presents. It's interesting how caught up we all are in our own tradition, in our own background, and in our own training. I was trained and brought up as a psychoanalyst before the theories that perhaps began to move, to fly ahead in the 50s with the ego psychology. I was brought up more with the id psychology. Jerry Frank had a very mixed training and he talks about demoralization in his very interesting case, which is that of an obsession. In his formulation, Jerry Frank says that his patient benefited because he helped her express her anger more assertively. But then he discovered, three years later, that he helped her because he made her feel like a real person. What was happening, as I see it, is a matter of not helping somebody to more assertively express anger; what happened is that he overcame the helpless, deteriorated, demoralized state that this woman was in. Whether he could do this by helping her assert herself, express anger, get her anger out, is an issue I'll talk about later. I think what happened is that in some way he overcame the demoralization, not that he helped somebody get the anger out.

Now, what is demoralization? As Dr. Frank expresses it, it is essentially a feeling of powerlessness, a feeling of helplessness, an inability to sustain one's functioning for a number of reasons that are described through our understanding of defensive networks which produce incapacities. This feeling of being unable to function, to control one's living whether it's on the inside or outside, becomes the demoralization issue.

Now, how we dress this up in formal language has become, I think, a great handicap in the development of theory. We've gotten caught up in language in the last ten years. Try reading some of the ego psychology texts. You may have a little less trouble than I do. I simply cannot follow it. I must be stupid. We've just heard presentations which are in language that you can grasp, you can understand, you can deal with, you can work with, you can argue with, and you can disagree with; but at least we have something we can deal with.

DR. MICHELS: Dr. Dewald, do you want to come to the defense of ego psychology?

DR. PAUL DEWALD: Yes, I come to the symposium as a classical psychoanalyst who has attempted to apply psychoanalytic thinking and theoretical assumptions to nonspecifically psychoanalytic therapeutic enterprises. I think I would take strong exceptions with Dr. Salzman and with Dr. Ornstein and I think that the problem is in the unfortuante tendency toward concretization and reification of a theory to a reality. Let me make it perfectly clear: there is no such thing as an ego. The ego is a convenient way of conceptualizing certain observable phenomena which exist only in the mind of the observer as he tries to order and make sense out of the behavior he is witnessing. The same would be true, for example, in the whole concept of structural theory. The structures do not exist. Structure and the concept of the structural theory reflect only a psychological way of looking at a cognitive way that the observer has of looking at the data of behavior and the various functions which compose behavior. I believe firmly in the construct of conflict and the awareness of the recognition that conflict can produce a variety of effects.

This leads me to two issues that I would like to emphasize. One, the idea of real change or structural change. What does that mean? It means only that a particular function (whether it's a small, specific, discreet function or whether it's a particular kind of organization of multiple functions that may be involved in a particular element or aspect of an individual's personality or behavior) has been significantly changed and altered so that what remains is essentially in a new state. The concept that is frequently used is structure building which somehow brings about a metaphoric image of bringing together inside the head a new set of images of oneself, images of someone else, recognition of or change in the perceptions that an individual has of the world around him. These are structures, so one has the concept, then, of change that can be from relatively superficial, relatively accessible, relatively derivative functions of the mind, all the way back to the basic intrapsychic fundamental core functions which determine so much of an individual's personality. In that sense, then, if an individual has changed in his or her behavior toward a spouse and that change persists within the individual, then I would say a structural change has occurred, although it may not be a change of a fundamental or basic set of functions.

I, therefore, would suggest, vis-à-vis Mrs. A., that in theory, the only way we are going to find out whether or not she has really changed in the sense of a permanent change, that is, in terms of her images of herself, in terms of her perception of others, in terms of her intrapsychic organization, is when Mr. A. dies. Does she then revert to her previous behavior? Does she, if she should seek a mate, choose a mate similar to Mr. A. as he was now at the end of the treatment or as he was at the beginning? If she chooses a mate that was like the one at the beginning, then we would say change did not occur. If she chooses a mate who is more like the man she is involved with now, we might say that it has.

Another point that I would make that runs through all the presentations is the role of transference. That's an issue that we can get into later perhaps, but I would point out this dichotomy between internal and external — between what goes on within the individuals and their response to the world, whether it's a marital partner, or, in Dr. Frank's terms, their assumptive orientation to the world. These to me are artificial dichotomies. The concept that I perceive as most useful is the idea that these are interactional. Each is involved with and is influenced by the other. The intrapsychic organization is the nature of the patient's internal needs, wishes, or fantasies; whatever influences the selection of those perceptions of the external world, or those events, or those situations, or people in the external world, and influences the individual's assumptions, using Dr. Frank's terms about them. The nature of the stress which the external world imposes upon the individual for conflict resolution and adaptation, in turn, may either enhance what goes on intrapsychically or oppose it. And may, therefore, be supportive of more effective adaptation or maybe in opposition to it. These are very complex issues but I think that there is a difficulty in trying to make this an either/or proposition.

Finally, I was somewhat confused, in hearing Dr. Frank's paper. It seems to me that he flip-flops back and forth between two different levels of discourse. The concept of neurophysiology and neurobiological substrates, I feel, is probably not at the same level of conceptual discussion as the idea of interaction in an interpersonal relationship or the elements of psychotherapy. I think we are a long way from being able to correlate the things that go on in an interpersonal relationship to what goes on in the brain. Hopefully some day — but not now.

DR. ALAN SKOLNIKOFF: In regard to this problem of change and whether it occurs inside or outside, I would like to continue with Dr. Dewald's comment and think about how to measure this change. If Mrs. A., for example, were to, after the death of Mr. A., move in with a friendly caring person or see a friendly caring therapist every other month, would that still constitute and continue to maintain her internalized self and object images? Would that constitute change? In other words, it seems to me that we're always dealing with the interaction of the environment, with the internal apparatus, the internal psychological apparatus. Often we can't measure or we don't know what the supports are out there, or we don't know what the influences of future stresses and traumas will be on the apparatus. This ambiguity appears in our speculations about Mrs. A. It also appears in Dr. Frank's example of the woman who said that he made her feel like a real person. That is to say, we don't know what it is that we are measuring at any given time. And I think the argument is really one that we have to constantly come back to. Let me tell you where I stand on it. It seems to me that in the example of Mrs. A. we could look at the moment when Mr. A. broke down, surprising her, and then she held his hand. Dr. Lewis asked: "Did Mrs. A. really have a need to defeat powerful others at that point?" Well, obviously there is no manifestation of that. She appears, at least in her overt behavior, to be holding his hand to be very supportive of his sudden breakdown and of his sudden tears at his despair that she'll never change. Now what we still infer is that perhaps beneath this facade, or beneath this overt behavior of her being very supportive of him, she has this unconscious need to defeat him, and perhaps that, in a modulated form, is what makes her change at least overtly. That doesn't necessarily mean that we have to explore that question in a psychoanalysis, or that we would say to ourselves, "This woman is too disturbed to work on this problem and just can't work on it regardless of what her pathology is." What she does with whatever that unconscious material is which we are observing the conscious manifestations of, we are working with the derivatives of what's going on and what's boiling up inside.

I really was very stimulated by Dr. Lewis' paper. I have little to disagree with about it. I think psychoanalysis does not have a sufficient explanation of the interaction between interpersonal and objective images of people on the outside and what that does to internal images. I think the whole issue of how we know what an internal image is, or an internal representation or an internal schemata is, is a very complex one, and when we get away from detailed observations of behaviors of patients we get more and more speculative and get into more and more levels of inference. I think Dr. Lewis very carefully helped us look through a variety of ways of looking at that material and he stayed with the changes in the overt behavior in Mrs. A. and we can't fault him for that.

Now, in regard to Dr. Frank's concept of demoralization, it seems to me to be a very useful concept. I've always subsumed such a concept under the concept of the reappearance of warded-off ego states that are very unpleasant. Also, I don't think that I would generalize and say that most patients that come to treatment have demoralization as a major feature. Perhaps so in certain settings. I would equate demoralization more with a continuum of depressive symptoms. But I see many patients in clinic settings, for example in universities, that come predominantly with more anxiety symptoms, and they are not demoralized at the point that they seek treatment. I think the social setting in which the treatment is offered determines what the state of mind of the patient is, and demoralization, I would think, would refer to some kind of social failure or some failure in a variety of aspects of that person's life. Let me give you an example of our setting at the University of California. In order to seek out some patients with anxiety, we freely let it be known that we were interested in studying work inhibitions, and we used the word studying. In this instance we got quite a few students who weren't demoralized at all. They were interested in studying their work inhibitions, but they weren't demoralized about them, and they would call themselves "patients," although the way we approached seeking them out was certainly not to seek out patients. In this setting we wouldn't use the term demoralization.

Further, I would agree with Dr. Dewald's statements about the neurological level that Dr. Frank described. I certainly couldn't attribute what he was describing to neurological factors although they might be at some point in the future. We might be able to, for example, differentiate neurotic conditions based on inborn constitutional factors. We can't do it today. I think from psychoanalytic research we often get very early information which tells us why certain things are happening and why a certain feature of the character develops. And I think these are, at least at this stage, the most that we have to go on.

DR. MICHELS: I'm going to turn to Dr. Lewis and Dr. Frank with no intent that they immediately resolve these questions. I'm going to ask them to say whatever they like to say now, but keep in mind that they'll have lots of time to talk later.

DR. JERRY LEWIS: I think the issues that my colleagues have commented upon are precisely the issues that the paper raises and are precisely the issues that intrigued me at this particular time. I think Dr. Dewald's suggestion that the proof of the pudding will be not in the eating, but in the death of Mr. A. and what happens subsequently, is something that is a concept that I find most congenial to my own thinking. At least insofar as the issue raised in the paper I presented. Those are not variables that we can experimentally manipulate, but have to wait and see.

Another comment I will make in regard to Dr. Dewald's comments — I'm terribly interested in the relationship, and I think it is a complex and reciprocal relationship, between what Dr. Frank refers to as our "assumptive world" and the nature of our ongoing interpersonal relationships. How does our assumptive world influence the way we live our life in a social, interpersonal context? But also, how does the living of that life feed back into our system of assumptions about the meaning of life and the nature of man and all of those primary issues that are at the heart of my thinking about assumptive worlds?

DR. JEROME FRANK: I am going to start somewhere else and talk about myself for a moment. My own background, I think, is relevant here. I'm the only member of this panel who came into psychiatry from psychology. So my formative thinking was not made by analytic institutes. It was by a man named Kurt Lewin, a psychologist in Germany, and he had several points, one of which is very important for our discussion today. His basic premise was that behavior is a function of persons, times, and environments, so that I'm in perfect agreement with everything that has been said about the continuing interaction of internal states or environmental states — that's what I meant by using that phrase, "open system," which is a poor one, I guess. I meant that everything, our psychological and physiological processes, is interacting all the time and our internal and external processes are always interacting. Kurt Lewin also made another quite important distinction which I found very valuable. He distinguished between historical cause and field cause. If I pick this up and drop it and it falls, the historical causes are: I reached out and picked it up, and raised it, and let go, and it dropped. The field causes are: the instant I let go, the law of gravity operated on it and it dropped. Now the psychoanalytic framework, you see, stresses historical causes. The Kurt Lewin framework, and the one I'm continuing to utilize, stresses the field cause — what's going on right now. So I came into psychiatry already immunized, you might say, against the psychoanalytic framework, and although I did have psychoanalysis and stuck it out in an institute for a while, it never took fully, and that will color my whole discussion, I'm afraid, from now on. Kurt had another point which was that concepts must be experimentally testable, so I'm impatient with concepts that you cannot, in any way, break down to a kind of experimental task, and that, to me, is the difference for many analytic concepts.

A final point, I think demoralization is both secondary and primary depending on the patient. If you believe, as I do, that we are an open system, then every mental state must have a physiological state and I quite agree that we don't know enough about neurophysiology. I was simply offering that to suggest this might explain why certain psychological symptoms are so unamenable to psychotherapy. Whatever their neurological substrate is, it isn't easily modifiable by symbolic inputs. That's really all I was trying to say here.

DR. MICHELS: When I first started going to seminars, I used to start from the beginning trying to learn something; and when I first started doing therapies, I used to start from the beginning trying to help my patients. Over the years I've learned that those are bad starting postures. When you start therapy you try to meet your patient — know him, know what he's like, get him to know what you're like, so that you can go on from there. And I've come to the point that when I come to seminars like this I start by trying to meet the panel, getting to know them, what their points of view are, what their terms and frames of reference are, what they seem like, their styles, so I'll be able to understand them from then on. I think we've done a marvelous job of getting to meet our panel this morning. They've each identified their turf, their frames of reference, their favorite metaphors and jokes, and those flash points where they begin to say, "Wait a minute, that isn't me at all, that isn't what I said"; and I think that should help us for the next day and a half.

Elements of Change and Cure

4

Paul A. Dewald

GENERAL CONCEPTS

Change in psychoanalysis is highly complicated and involves a multivariable situation. It is not an all or nothing phenomenon, nor does it occur only after a particular elapsed time or phase, nor does it usually occur suddenly or dramatically. Change is more likely to occur in a continuing, at times barely perceptible, spiraling fashion, in which one element of the process influences another,

This chapter is an abbreviated version of Dewald, P. A., "Elements of Change and Cure in Psychoanalysis," *Archives of General Psychiatry*, 40:89-95, © 1983 American Medical Association.

sometimes sequentially and sometimes simultaneously, leading to the unfolding of an ever-deepening and expanding process (Dewald, 1972).

Changes can be conceptualized as *facilitative* versus *definitive*. By facilitative I am referring to those components in the psycho-analytic process which must necessarily occur in order to provide the frame and field, as well as the vehicles and tools, for patient and analyst eventually to initiate and sustain the processes which lead to definitive cure.

As illustrative of facilitative change I would include such elements as the establishment of the psychoanalytic situation; the unfolding of a therapeutic alliance and a regressive transference neurosis; the intensification of the transference experience through the maintenance of appropriate transference abstinence by the analyst; the offering by the analyst of appropriately timed inter-ventions and interpretations; the recognition and reduction of the patient's use of various tactical resistances (Dewald, 1980); the patient's increasingly direct exposure to and tolerance of affects, drives, and previously unconscious fantasies; and the acquisition by the patient of deeper and progressively more personalized under-standing and insight.

All these issues are crucial aspects of the overall psycho-analytic process. Each occupies a considerable amount of the time, technique, and energy, which both patient and analyst devote to the work. Their importance as necessary precursors to the process of cure cannot be emphasized enough.

Out of these changes emerge the more *definitive* elements in the analysis which lead ultimately to cure. As illustrations of defini-tive change I would include such process elements as internalization and identification; the reliving and ultimate resolution of important developmental crises; the increase in psychic continuity (both longitudinally and cross-sectionally); the applications by the patient of insight gained; and the renunciation of inappropriate infantile and childhood wishes, namely the overcoming of the *strategic* resistances.

Many discussions of the curative factors in psychoanalysis have emphasized the importance of recovering repressed material, the acquisition of insight, and the working through of the transference neurosis. It is my thesis that important as these factors may be, the analytic process is far more complex, and that in addition to intrapsychic elements it involves important interpersonal experiences that contribute significantly to the final process.

In the clinical situation the distinction between the intrapsychic transference and the interpersonal interactional elements of the relationship may not always be clear and sharp. Transference phenomena influence the selection of perceptions of interpersonal elements in the situation as well as the emotional significance which those perceptions have for the patient. And reality experiences in the interpersonal sphere may activate a variety of transference responses. However, in spite of such overlapping, there is a schematic advantage in separating these two elements in the total relationship.

Both facilitative and definitive changes occur gradually, but the rate of change tends to be geometric rather than linear in its progression; and the major thrust of definitive change often occurs only in the late middle and termination phases of the work.

THE INTERPERSONAL RELATIONSHIP

There are a variety of elements in the interpersonal interactions between patient and analyst by which the analysis comes to represent a new and unique type of object relationship for the patient. These include: the constancy of the analyst's interest and acceptance, regardless of the type of material which the patient presents; a high degree of reliability in the analyst in regard to keeping appointments, duration of the sessions, and structure of the situation; the analyst's systematic attempt to put the patient's welfare foremost in the situation between them and not to use the patient for his or her own personal needs; the analyst's suspension of moral value judgments and willingness not to require that the patient conform to any particular standard of behavior determined by the analyst; the analyst's demonstration via the interventions he or she makes of the capacity for empathy, insight, understanding, and acceptance, thus relieving the patient of a previous sense of isolation and alienation in regard to his own thoughts, wishes, fantasies, and earlier feelings; the patient's opportunity now openly and directly "to speak the unspeakable" to someone who not only tolerates its being spoken, but demonstrates an active interest and desire to understand its meanings; and the analyst's maintenance of a holding environment (Modell, 1979) through interventions which protect the patient from disruptive levels of unpleasure or disorganization.

In these forms of appropriate analytic behavior, the analyst provides a type of early parent-child relationship and experience. Greenacre (1954) has commented on the difficulties for patients caused by the "tilt" in the analytic relationship. I would point out that by maintaining the appropriate classical psychoanalytic position, stance and activity, and by permitting oneself to be used by the patient as a transference object, the analyst contributes to a new unique kind of new relationship, "tilted" heavily in favor of the patient's ultimate well-being.

During any analysis there may be prolonged periods of bitter transference frustration and resultant hostility, negativism, withdrawal, contempt or criticism of the analyst by the patient. The fact that these responses and behaviors do not cause the analyst to retaliate, reject, or otherwise move out of the analytic position offers the patient another evidence of a unique form of acceptance.

INTERNALIZATION AND IDENTIFICATION

Such experiences result in progressive internalization and identification with the analyst by the patient, including the patient's development of self-analyzing functions; the shift in the patient's ego-ideal toward a more active willingness for introspection and the acceptance of psychic truth; a greater tolerance in consciousness of primary process thinking and affects; and a model of interpersonal activity involving empathy, altruism, and constancy. Although some elements of identfication with the analyst are defensive and need eventually to be analyzed and given up by the patient, some of the characteristics just enumerated are permanent and tend to persist after the analysis is over.

REGRESSIVE RELIVING OF DEVELOPMENTAL CRISES

The hallmark of an analysis is the unfolding conscious recognition and affective participation by the patient in the emergence of a regressive transference neurosis. In this paradigm, the patient ultimately experiences in consciousness many of the regressive infantile and early childhood core fantasies, wishes, object choices, defenses, adaptive organizations, and expectations. While these phenomena are *not the same* as the original developmental processes, they probably represent an approximation of the patient's infantile and childhood developmental psychic experiences, now reported and modified as actual "here and now" phenomena by a verbal adult.

Simultaneously or in oscillation, as part of the therapeutic alliance, the adult patient is also aware of the "as if" aspects of this situation and set of experiences, and is willing and able to tolerate the unpleasure, "danger" and distortions induced by the transference regression in hopes of ultimately being cured of the neurotic process.

Whatever the level of regression and vivid immediacy of experience of the infantile and early childhood phenomena, the analyst seeks to maintain his or her analytic posture in the face of the patient's multiple transference-inspired attempts to elicit a gratifying, seductive, punitive, rejecting, sado-masochistic, or other inappropriate reaction. In spite of the patient's transference expectations and demands, the analyst maintains abstinence for the transference wishes; continues the empathic interpretation of the meaning, significance, and relatedness of the patient's material; demonstrates continued acceptance and tolerance of the patient without judgment or prejudice; and continues in the primary concern for the patient and the patient's perceptions of the earlier childhood relationships, fantasies, wishes, traumata, and methods of adaptation.

This maintenance of transference and countertransference abstinence by the analyst serves several important functions. Frustration of derivative wishes tends to promote further regressive awareness and to intensify the pressures for wish fulfillment. Such abstinence also makes the situation "safe" for the patient to give full verbal and affective expression to previously repressed wishes, without having to be immediately responsible for action or reaction. It also sets a model for the patient in regard to the solid distinction between feelings and fantasies on the one hand and acts on the other.

At the level of the regression occurring in the transference neurosis, the analyst now represents a new and different object. While the patient's transference-induced expectations of the analyst persist, the patient's current regressive experience of the analyst in the anticipated dangerous relationship is not in keeping with the transference expectations.

In that sense, the patient now has an opportunity partly to relive some of his or her early developmental conflicts with a person who is responding differently than did the original objects, either in reality as they actually responded or in the patient's fantasy, as imagined. In this way the current regressive experience of the analyst represents a fresh or new reality for the patient occurring at the level of the transference-induced regression. Additionally, in spite of the regression, the patient also has available an adult capacity for reality testing and for options in regard to the resolution of the previous developmental crises, alternatives which were not available to the child at the time of his original development.

These two sets of perceptions in the patient's regressive transference experiences (the repetitive transference expectations and wishes, and the new experience with the analyst at that level of regression) provide a differential set of phenomena which must be reconciled by the more mature, self-observing, integrative, and synthetic functions which are part of the patient's activities in the therapeutic alliance. The process of reconciling the differences between these two forms of experience at the level of regression which the analysis has induced is a significant definitive component in the production of change.

It is a common analytic experience that a transference-induced process is activated during which the patient simultaneously reexperiences a pleasurable and/or painful childhood organization; regressively relives it; observes him- or herself at the same time from a more mature adult perspective; and introduces that more mature perspective into the simultaneous reliving of the old trauma at the regressive level, and the beginning achievement of a new and different pattern of resolution.

These phenomena also allow us to understand more clearly why countertransference interferences with the function of the analyst are so disruptive of analytic progress. When the patient in the regressive transference experience can provoke in the analyst a response which is in keeping with the patient's childhood or infantile expectations and which is a repetition of the fantasies or actual ways in which other individuals have responded in the past, the differential between those expectations and the current regressive experience is not wide enough to permit change to occur. The present experience with the analyst then becomes another repetition of the past, and the patient's original neurotic expectations, perceptions, and distortions are again confirmed and strengthened.

ACCESS TO AFFECTS, DRIVES, AND FANTASIES

An important element of change, which is initially facilitative but eventually is also definitive, occurs as the patient progressively achieves access to deeper, more direct and basic awareness of affects, drives and the previously unconscious fantasies by which they are experienced and expressed. This change results from repeated exposure to initially "dangerous" psychic experiences which for the patient are threatening and against which multiple automatic and unconscious adaptive and defensive functions have been directed. The patient repeatedly recognizes such mental contents and finds through experience that such feelings and fantasies can be allowed into the consciousness while controlling access to action. The patient consolidates confidence in the difference between expression in verbal form and destructive or dangerous activity, and progressively the awareness and experience of affects and drives becomes less dangerous and threatening.

An important element in this process is the patient's observation of the analyst and the analyst's comfort with such phenomena, a willingness to discuss and try to understand them in verbal form, an implied faith in the patient's capacities for control and a suspension of moralizing judgment and punishment for such impulses and fantasies. Once again by maintaining an analytic position, the analyst thus also serves as a significant new model for identification by the patient in regard to ego and superego functions in regard to such psychic processes.

In this repeated spiraling process the patient experiences the "dangerous situation" in fantasy, accompanied by signal or neurotic anxiety or other affects, and leading initially to characteristic unconscious adaptive or defensive operations. The analyst and analytic process encourage the patient to suspend these defensive operations, to undergo further intensification and direct experience of the earlier danger situations and fantasies, and to tolerate the anxiety which accompanies them for progressively longer intervals. This in turn leads to an improved capacity for mastery of the anxiety and also simultaneously for better perception of the difference between thought and action. The final effect is an enhanced confidence for and control of those stimuli which still evoke the signal of anxiety, a decrease in the number of such stimuli and situations, and a substitution of conscious for previously unconscious adaptive mechanisms and functions. These changes in ego functions are also accompanied by modification of the superego and the ego-ideal, inasmuch as the individual is now capable of tolerating without undue guilt or shame and as part of self-image elements which were previously threatening, unacceptable or intolerable.

THE USES OF INSIGHT

One of the results of the analytic process is that the patient achieves a new level of personal insight and understanding in regard to self, past history and traumatic experiences, and the repetition in the present of now outmoded and no-longer age-appropriate fantasies and interactions with earlier key people. A discussion of the pathogenic significance of primitive, unconscious, intrapsychic fantasy systems is beyond the scope of this presentation (see Arlow, 1969), but the insight which is acquired includes the detailed elaboration of the origins and varying forms of the pathogenic fantasies, their organization and their effects.

Insight by itself, however, does not produce change. It is how the patient applies and uses that insight to modify and resolve pre-existing conflicts that determines whether or not change will occur.

But the acquisition of insight now permits the patient, from the standpoint of adult reality testing, to expose the details of the specifically pathogenic unconscious fantasy systems to the corrective influence of adult reality testing, thereby gradually changing the preexisting pathogenic fantasy to a relatively harmless memory.

In the psychoanalytic situation the patient has an opportunity regressively to relive some of the developmental crises he or she was unable to resolve successfully as a child. In doing so this time various adult mental functions are available which have developed since the original crisis. There is also the empathic support, guidance, control, constancy and attitude of the analyst, and the patient will not have to cope with the perceived danger situations alone. In spite of transference expectations of conflict, this time the environment (analytic situation and analyst) is an understanding participant in the achievement of resolution and mastery.

TERMINATION AND RENUNCIATION

One of the major definitive processes leading to cure is the resolution of the transference neurosis which occurs during the termination phase of the analysis. The analytic process has deliberately activated a set of experiences within the patient, leading to the investment in the analyst and the analytic situation of the regressive infantile and early childhood wishes, yearnings, object choices, hopes, and fantasies of fulfillment, as well as the various reactions of pain, disappointment, and aggression at the frustrations which are involved.

In the termination phase the analyst represents simultaneously the original infantile and early childhood objects and the yearnings for satisfaction in those relationships; the objects of transference frustration and activated aggressive and destructive wishes; the newly experienced regressive object in relationship to whom the patient has more successfully relived some of the significant developmental conflicts and phases; the professional therapist with whom the mature elements of the patient's personality have cooperated in the therapeutic venture; and the newly internalized object with whom both the regressive and mature components of the patient's personality have undergone a variety of new and unique experiences.

All of these elements of the relationship must be voluntarily modified and/or renounced by the patient if a final cure of the underlying neurosis is to occur. In the typical process of grief, mourning, and renunciation which occurs in regard to the analyst and the analytic relationship during termination, the patient is simultaneously renouncing claims on the original objects and the relationships that they represented.

By giving up claims to and yearnings for the fulfillment of libidinal and aggressive infantile and childhood strivings and the objects to which they are attached, the patient undergoes a significant psychic maturation. The impulses and yearnings may then be modified in keeping with the patient's developing adult status and currently available age-appropriate objects and activities, now enabling him or her to express drives and affects in realistically satisfying and conflict-free forms.

While the original infantile and early childhood fantasies, yearnings, and wishes are never fully renounced and persist in even the healthiest of individuals, their intensity and peremptoriness are significantly reduced. There can then occur a controlled access to the basic core of the individual's psychic life, enabling freer, less conflicted and ultimately more realistically fulfilling forms of satisfaction of basic human needs. These processes of maturation represent the ultimate definitive phenomena of change and cure in psychoanalysis. And these maturational processes of renunciation and reorganization reach their greatest intensity during the termination phase, and are the final common expression and effect of all the earlier facilitative and definitive curative elements of the psycoanalytic process.

The elements of change described for classical psychoanalysis are also applicable to the process of change in psychoanalytic psychotherapy. In another contribution (Dewald, 1978) I elaborated upon the differences between resolution of core psychic conflict as it occurs in psychoanalysis, and derivative psychic conflict which is the usual focus in psychoanalytic psychotherapy. Core issues reflect conflict or arrest in development which occurred in and are a direct function of the infantile and early childhood phases of the individual's life. Derivative conflicts reflect processes which are an expression of the basic or core issues as these are manifested and experienced in later developmental phases from latency, adolescent and earlier adult life situations and experiences. Derivative issues and conflicts tend to be closer to conscious awareness, organized more in keeping with secondary process fantasy, experience, and thought, and they tend to be expressed through memories, experiences, and psychic elaborations of issues which occurred later in the individual's life and development.

In psychoanalytic psychotherapy (as contrasted with psychoanalysis) the focus of therapeutic attention, work, reconstruction, recall, and experience tends to be at the level of derivative psychic phenomena and conflict. In psychotherapy the derivative areas of development and conflict represent the level of exploration that is sought; and to accomplish this the therapist seeks to limit the intensity of regression, the extent to which transference emerges (transference reactions, in contrast to a transference neurosis which is sought in psychoanalysis) and the nature of the psychic experiences which occur between patient and therapist. The same issues and processes described earlier as elements of change or cure in psychoanalysis occur in psychotherapy but at less intensive, extensive, or regressive levels of psychological experience. Psychoanalytic psychotherapy represents a form of applied psychoanalysis in which significant but more focal degrees of change are possible as a result of the treatment process.

REFERENCES

Arlow, Jacob A. (1969). Unconscious fantasy and disturbances of conscious experience. *Psychoanal Q*, 38:1-37.

Dewald, Paul A. (1972). *The Psychoanalytic Process*. New York; Basic Books.

_____ (1980). The handling of resistances in adult psychoanalysis. *Int J Psychoanal*, 61:61-69.

Gill, Merton M. (1979). The analysis of the transference. *J Am Psychoanal Assn*, Supplement 27:263-288.

Greenacre, Phyllis (1954). The role of transference: practical considerations in relation to psychoanalytic therapy. *J Am Psychol Assn*, 2:671-684.

Modell, Arnold (1979). The action of the holding environment. *J Am Psychoanal Assn*, 27:637-642.

Dewald, Paul A. (1978). The Process of Change in Psychoanalytic Psychotherapy. *Arch Gen Psychiat* 35:535-542.

5

Some Curative Factors and Processes in the Psychoanalytic Psychotherapies

Paul H. Ornstein

INTRODUCTION

There are six different presentations on the same topic at this symposium — six different clinical and theoretical vantage points, from which the curative process of psychotherapy is to be illuminated. This makes it necessary (and I hope also helpful) for me to begin with a few introductory statements in order to put my broad and sketchy overview of what is curative in the psychoanalytic psychotherapies into a proper perspective.

I speak of the psychoanalytic psychotherapies, which include: brief, focal psychotherapy; long-term intensive psychoanalytic psychotherapy; and psychoanalysis. I place all of these on a continuum.

These therapeutic modalities are properly viewed as fundamentally more similar and, therefore, in fact, on a continuum — rather than as sharply delineated, distinct forms of treatment — *if* the same personality theory, the same theory of psychopathology, the same method of treatment (namely, understanding and interpretation), and the same theory of cure guide the therapist in his or her interventions. Generally speaking, each of the three treatment settings give rise to different kinds of treatment processes and (presumably) to three different kinds of results. Each treatment setting will allow certain aspects and a certain degree of depth of the transference to emerge: (1) in focal psychotherapy only a small segment and a limited degree of depth might be mobilized; (2) in intensive psychoanalytic psychotherapy a much larger segment and a greater degree of depth; and finally, (3) in psychoanalysis — hopefully — the fuller pathognomonic transference will emerge and will take the center-stage in the process of working through.

By emphasizing the similarities, I do not wish to minimize or blur the quantitative and qualitative differences that may arise, but for our present purpose, namely, for the delineation of the curative factors and processes in all these treatment forms, the similarities are of greater fundamental significance. This will permit me to focus predominantly on the psychoanalytic process but it applies to others as well.

My working assumption is, that each patient-therapist encounter sets off a process that unfolds between them and in each of them. As far as the curative factors are concerned, these reside within "the process," which is triggered for its unfolding by the encounter. This process overshadows the therapist's manifest "technique" in its importance for cure.

To put this differently, the three treatment modalities I speak of as the psychoanalytic psychotherapies are unified by a primary emphasis upon the process that develops between patient and therapist and within each of them. The psychoanalytic psychotherapies are not separated into distinct modalities of treatment by a primary emphasis upon the technique the therapist uses. Thus, we may speak of a process-oriented or a technique-oriented delineation of the psychotherapies. I use here the process-oriented approach exclusively. In such a process-oriented approach all three psychoanalytic treatment forms are essentially (and in spite of their differences) of one cloth.

What is this process that unifies the psychoanalytic psycho-therapies, lends them their respective therapeutic efficacies or curative factors, and is of far greater significance than what we refer to as the therapist's "technique"?

This "therapeutic process" refers to the unique experiences of the patient, which are mobilized in any therapist-patient relation-ship and originate from the unique constellation of the patient's inner needs and the therapist's responses to them. This process encompasses both the nonspecific (empathy, nonjudgmental atti-tudes, etc.) and the specific (conflict resolution, transmuting inter-nalization, etc.) curative factors in each of the psychoanalytic treatment modalities.

There is a growing and increasingly more wide-spread con-sensus among psychoanalysts today, which holds that the trans-ference is central to the treatment process in all psychoanalytic psychotherapies.

Although transference arises spontaneously in any form of treatment, in fact, it arises in any extra-therapeutic, everyday close relationship as well — most particularly in friendships and marriages — and is, therefore, rightly considered ubiquitous. But when it emerges in the psychoanalytic psychotherapies, transference acquires a special quality, role, and function through the therapeutic regres-sion and through the psychoanalyst's responses to it. These responses essentially consist of its acceptance, understanding, and explanation, regardless of the treatment setting. Only the nature of the under-standing and explanation varies with the treatment setting.

The setting itself, as already stated, contributes to what will emerge in the transference, but its special quality will arise out of the fact, that the transference is *not* deliberately provoked, or fostered, or actively mobilized; nor is it suppressed, ignored, or otherwise bypassed. It is allowed to emerge within a neutral, non-judgmental, accepting, and development-enhancing climate of optimum frustration. It is this optimum frustration, this key condi-tion for structure building in infancy and childhood, as well as in the analytic treatment process, that can only occur reliably and predictably in the analytic forms of therapeutic relationship. It cannot occur in those extratherapeutic relationships that I mentioned earlier — for a variety of reasons. Furthermore, nowhere else does the patient have as complete a chance for the mobilization of his transference, without similar transference demands being placed upon him in friendship or marriage. It is this complete centering upon the patient and his transference experiences in the analytic treatment process that invites the regressive remobilization of those pathognomonic transferences or their derivatives, that then provide the basis for the unique healing process offered by the psychoanalytic psychotherapies.

Before I can even briefly survey the nonspecific and specific curative factors, I will have to define further the psychoanalytic therapeutic process in conjunction with the nature of health and illness, the method of responding to what the patient brings to the therapeutic setting, and the way we envision a "cure" in such a context.

The Therapeutic Process and the Transference

In Webster's *Third New International Dictionary* (1961, p. 1808), the following definitions of process are given: ". . . the action of moving forward progressively from one point to another on the way to completion; the action of passing through continuing development from a beginning to a contemplated end; the action of continuous going along through each of succession of acts, events or developmental stages; an actual, progressively continuing operation or development marked by a series of graduate changes that succeed one another in a relatively fixed way and lead toward a particular result or end."

In relation to the therapeutic process in psychoanalysis, Kris (1956, p. 445) has offered this definition: "A distinct property of psychoanalysis is its character as a process with a notion, however loosely defined, of progressive development over time in a definite direction."

I can now expand in the remainder of this presentation these broad definitions with the specifics of the psychoanalytic therapeutic process, from the vantage point of contemporary psychoanalytic self psychology.

What is this progressive development with a definite direction and a contemplated end? What is developing and where does such a development lead?

The Nature of Health and Illness — A Developmental and Psychogenetic Perspective

From the developmental and psychogenetic perspective offered by self psychology the definition of mental health and illness should be made clinically relevant by a brief outline of the developmental origins and the ultimate structure of the bipolar self.

The point to be stressed here for contrast and comparison is that classical psychoanalysis derives psychic development from the clash of forces of the primary drives with the socializing demands of the parental imagoes, as the earliest representatives of the social environment. Self psychology derives psychic development from within the self-selfobject matrix, where the rudimentary self and its empathic selfobject constitute the primal unit of psychological experience. Health and illness can only be understood from within this matrix, since we need selfobjects from birth to death; early we need archaic selfobjects for the maintenance of cohesiveness and structure building and mature selfobjects for the continued maintenance of our vigor, vitality, and creativeness. The self can therefore never be viewed in isolation or separately from its archaic or mature selfobject matrix.

The early task of development and maturation is to form a cohesive nuclear bipolar self, which guarantees a relatively stable, internal self-regulation. Once the cohesive self is fully formed and structuralized, a process which never ends and is therefore an open rather than a closed system, its central life-long task is to afford the realization of that "inner design" which is laid down in the structures of the nuclear self. The two main lines of the development of the self that originate in the self-selfobject matrix should now follow:

In one line of development, under optimum circumstances, the grandiose-exhibitionistic self, in its mirroring selfobject-matrix, becomes the pole of *self-assertive ambitions*, with the following major functional tasks or capacities: (1) the capacity for a relatively autonomous self-esteem regulation; (2) the capacity for the enjoyment of our mental and physical activities; and (3) the capacity to pursue our goals and purposes.

In the other line of development the idealized parental imago, in its idealized selfobject-matrix, becomes the pole of *internalized values and guiding ideals*, with the following major functional tasks or capacities: (1) the capacity for self-soothing and self-calming – internal tension regulation; (2) the capacity for the containment and appropriate channeling of our affects and drive needs; (3) the capacity for enthusiasm and for the idealization of our values and guiding principles.

Between these two poles of the bipolar self are our innate skills and talents, which are activated by our ambitions on the one hand and our ideals and principles on the other.

This schematic outline of the development of the bipolar self already implies both the structural and functional definitions of mental health and illness, which should now be made explicit.

To start with a broad definition of illness, clinical experience will immediately guide us to recognize the various disorders in either or both poles of the bipolar self. We see mild to severe disturbances in self-esteem regulation; mild to severe inability to enjoy mental or physical activities, accompanied by inner emptiness and despair; mild to severe inability to actively pursue goals and purposes – all based on varying degrees of deficiency in the structuralization of the pole of the ambitions. We see mild to severe inability for self-soothing or self-calming; or the containment and channeling of affects and drive needs, that is, a broad lack of capacity for tension regulation, which may lead to addictions, perversions, and criminal activities – all based on various degrees of deficiency in the structuralization of the pole of ideals and values. All these disorders in either or both poles of the self attest to the developmental arrests or derailments and, result in the incomplete, inadequate or faulty structuralization of the self. Thus illness is a multi-faceted and variable incapacity (based on conflicts or deficits) in the realm of self-assertive ambition or in the realm of ideals and values, which inhibits or otherwise interferes with the unfolding of innate talents and skills or interferes with their appropriate use, once they have developed. Psychopathology, according to this view, is always considered from a developmental and psychogenetic perspective. And its cure can only be envisaged from the very same perspective. In other words, if pathology is ultimately a form of developmental arrest of deficiency, and conflicts develop secondarily around such arrests or deficiencies, cure has to provide a process for belated "structure building" and/or "structural change," as the expressions of belated maturation and growth.

Health, on the other hand, is the outcome of a felicitous developmental process, it is a multi-faceted and variable capacity to put one's innate skills and talents in the service of one's self-assertive ambitions, in keeping with one's internal guiding ideals and values. Thus, structural completeness of the self and the functional freedom with which it may put its skills and talents in the service of its nuclear ambitions and ideals characterize mental health. The correlated cure was thought to have been achieved when a well-functioning connection ". . . in the center of the personality, from the pole of ambitions, through skills and talents, to the pole of ideals has been established and the unfolding of a productive life has thus become a realizable possibility" (Kohut, 1981).

This definition needs further expansion and revision, since it implies that structure formation leads to independence from (archaic) selfobjects and that therefore the replacement of selfobjects by selfstructure constituted the essence of health, and in psychoanalysis the essence of cure.

These conceptions of health and cure derived from the study of the psychoanalysis of narcissistic personality disorders. The inclusion of the neuroses in this study led Kohut (1978) to recognize that the life-long need for selfobjects also required a modification of the concepts of health and cure.

While structure formation via transmuting internalization is still a major part of the developmental process toward health, and in the analytic process toward cure, we now had to recognize that ". . . the gradual acquisition of the ability to maintain the self within the matrix of mature self-selfobject relationships, i.e., the acquisition of empathic contact with selfobjects, is the essence of the psychoanalytic cure."

It now remains for us to indicate how this cure is brought about in the psychoanalytic psychotherapies.

The Analyst's Responsiveness and the Nature of the Curative Process

It follows from what has been said so far, that psychoanalytic therapy has as its fundamental task to create a climate in which the inherent developmental tendency, within each person, hitherto thwarted, derailed or arrested, can now resume its progressive, forward moving unfolding, toward a contemplated (hypothetical) end-point.

Kohut (1981) described this process of establishing a climate of optimum frustration extensively and focused on the three steps that brought about cure: (1) clearing away the obstacles to the remobilization of the transference (defense analysis); (2) the unfolding of the pathognomonic, regressive transference; and (3) — "the essential step, because *it* defines the aim and the result of cure: it is the opening of a path of empathy between self and selfobject, specifically, the establishment of empathic in-tuneness between self and selfobject on adult, mature levels — the opening of a channel, which now permanently takes the place of the formerly regressed or split off archaic narcissistic relationship, of the bondage that had formerly tied the archaic self to the archaic selfobject." The emphasis here is on the change from archaic to mature selfobjects and not on the final relinquishment of selfobjects altogether.

How is this belated structuralization of the self and the attainment of the functional freedom of the self brought about in psychoanalysis? How is the replacement of archaic with mature selfobjects accomplished? How is the claimed essential step in the curative process, namely, the opening of a path of empathy between self and selfobject made within the psychoanalytic process?

The archaic and oedipal selfobject transferences provide the context within which the necessary, belated developmental steps can be taken. Kohut (1981) describes how analysis can recreate the favorable conditions for structure building in the following ways: (1) by reactivation of a childhood need (in conflict neuroses, an instinctual wish), and optimal frustration via (2) nonfulfillment (abstinence), since the needs and wishes are not directly responded to, and (3) substitution of the indirect need fulfillment by the establishment of a bond of empathy between analyst and analyzand.

Thus, in a climate of overall acceptance and a pervasive nonjudgmental attitude, there is a favorable context for the systematic application of what Kohut (1981) calls the "basic therapeutic unit": (1) understanding and (2) explaining.

On the level of understanding the analyst establishes an empathic bond that is curative in the psychoanalytic sense, in which such an understanding may lead to structure-building, because it exposes the patient to a modicum of optimum frustration (no understanding can ever be complete or perfect) and thus contributes to the laying down of new defect-filling, or cohesion-firming psychic structures. Understanding and legitimizing a reactivated childhood need or wish in the transference is still frustrating, since the analyst does not respond to the need or wish by acting upon it, which makes this, then, optimal frustration rather than optimal gratification. This is Kohut's (1981) argument here: why empathic understanding in itself constitutes – and has always constituted – an aspect or a part of psychoanalytic cure (however decried or deemphasized in certain quarters).

Now, what about the second step of analytic activity – the step of explaining or interpretation? What are the additional benefits that accrue from this second step, and how does it complete this two step-process of analytic cure? The second step might be viewed as consisting of two substeps – dynamic and genetic explanations of the patient's transference experiences. Explanation deepens the patient's own empathic-accepting grasp of himself; it strengthens his trust in the reality and reliability of the bond of empathy that is being established between himself and the analyst, by putting him (the patient) in touch with the full depth and breadth of the analyst's understanding of him. In addition, through this step of explaining, the temporary or more evanescent benefits of empathic understanding will be transcended and the analyzand will begin to use these insights to weather the storm in the process of working through.

As Kohut (1981) offers his explanation of psychoanalytic cure, he depends on two major self psychological assumptions:

(1) The first concerns the functional yield that we expect to result from the expansion and the firming up of self structures. (2) The second has to do with the assumption that we can best understand analytic cure in analogy with successful early development, that is, with the laying down of psychological structures via optimum frustration.

If we hold fast to these two assumptions, a variety of questions regarding analytic cure might be answered. It will be clear, for example, that the more accurately our theories correspond to the psychic realities that underlie our patients' disturbances, the closer will our interpretations come to providing for the patient, in an adult setting and in an adult form, the optimum frustrations that the flawed self-selfobject responses of early life had failed to supply.

This might easily be misconstrued again, as corrective emotional experience. Kohut (1981) is aware of this and says that the only way analysts could avoid this sort of gratifying that relates to the patient's need to be understood, is by consistently confronting them with erroneous, inaccurate or untimely interpretations — a technique, no analyst would deliberately apply, I believe.

We should note, however, that the third step in the curative process, the opening of a path of empathy between the self and its self-object, is defined as the essential step, but this does not preclude the fact that gaining knowledge may and often does contribute in a subsidiary or secondary fashion to the overall beneficial results of psychoanalysis. Self psychology does not see the essence of the curative process to lie per se in the cognitive sphere, that is, in the attainment of insight, whether we express this in the terms of the topographic model of Freud as "the unconscious becomes conscious," or in the sense of the later structural model of "where id was, ego shall be". In other words, self psychology claims that the essence of the curative process cannot be defined, at least not per se by reference to the expansion of the realm of awareness, nor by reference to the increased ability of the psychic apparatus to modify the drives. Again, self psychology does not see the essence of the curative process primarily in the expansion of the domain of the ego.

The increased capacity to channel and contain drive needs, which may well precede, accompany, or follow the curative process, does not in itself bring about the cure.

I have omitted the discussion of other important component elements of the therapeutic process for brevity's sake and because I assume that there will be overlapping statements by some of the other presenters. In other words, I have omitted what we might be able to agree upon, in order to highlight those areas where we might differ.

NOTES

Kohut, Heinz and Wolf, Ernest S. (1978) "The disorders of self and their treatment: an outline" International Journal of Psychoanalysis 59, 413-425

Kohut, Heinz (1981) "How does analysis cure?" Unpublished manuscript

Kris, Ernst (1956) "On some vicissitudes of insight in psychoanalysis" International Journal of Psychoanalysis 37, 445

Webster's Third New International Dictionary (1961) G. and C. Merriam Co., Springfield, Mass., p. 1808

6

Psychoanalytic Points of View: Dialogue II

DR. ROBERT MICHELS: We've narrowed the domain of discussion to psychoanalysis and psychoanalytic types of psychotherapy. As the introduction to this discussion of two different theories of how psychoanalysis works and how psychoanalytic cure is going to be conceptualized, I remind you that Dr. Frank told us earlier that there is no very impressive evidence that it makes any difference what kind of therapy the therapist does technically. We hear, in passing, discussions by both of the presenters about the difference between psychoanalysis and psychotherapy. And we hear some parallels as well as some important differences. Dr. Dewald refers to the nonspecific and the facilitating and the definitive aspects of therapeutic technique. Dr. Ornstein refers to the nonspecific

67

and the specific aspects and I think there is considerable overlap between those two dichotomies that each establishes. They both talk about the central role of the relationship with the therapist and place in the center of their discussion how to see what goes on in the human relationship of therapist and patient in tension with, in opposition with, in coordination with the insight or information that is transferred from therapist to patient in the process of treatment. I'm not sure of this, but to my ear Dr. Dewald, speaking clearly from a classical psychoanalytic position, goes very far toward emphasizing the importance of interpersonal interactions, as well as insight as a coordinate in the therapeutic process and veers very close to being vulnerable to the accusation of almost hinting at a corrective emotional experience, an accusation that Dr. Ornstein forcibly protects himself from by an advanced defense. Dr. Dewald advocates frustration of the transference wishes, if I hear him, and makes no apology or compromise on that. Dr. Ornstein talks about optimal frustration which could sound like it allows a little bit of gratification because total frustration might not be optimal anymore. I want to hear him talk about that as we go on. However, I think core to the differences between the views they suggest is, on the one hand, Dr. Ornstein's insistence that the basic model of treatment is borrowed from the model of psychic development in which treatment must be understood in developmental terms. In effect, all pathology for Ornstein is fixation or developmental arrest. I believe Dr. Dewald has a regressive rather than fixative notion of much pathology, and would see treatment as repairing a fully developed system which has a defect in it, with regression being the therapeutic technique to allow the repair rather than a maneuver to facilitate arrested growth. Some of Dr. Dewald's patients are fully grown but have something wrong. All of Dr. Ornstein's patients are not fully grown or, if I understand his model, the resumption of development doesn't really offer much in the way of possibility.

Now, from the head shakes of the two, they're going to explain to me why I'm wrong. I believe the difference between fixation and regression as the dominant model of psychopathology is central here. I would note that both Ornstein and Dewald emphasize the regressive development of the transference neuroses. That's not the issue.

Finally, we try to understand what it is that happens besides insight. Dr. Dewald sticks to fairly comfortable and descriptive language, the interpersonal relationship — language unfamiliar to most analysts, at least those who didn't train in the Washington area, but language that describes the therapeutic encounter. Dr. Ornstein invokes a concept which is appealing but not always precise, that of empathy. He feels that empathy is vital, central, the essence of what happens in cure. Now, I know what empathy means as a mode of perception, as a way of knowing something, but he clearly means much more than that. He means empathy as something that goes on in an interactive two-way process in treatment and, therefore, although he reads us the dictionary when he's talking about certain other things, he's written his own dictionary on this one and we'll have to get him to expound more on it. But before we give either of the speakers a chance to reply to all that, I'm going to ask the others to say a word.

DR. ALAN SKOLNIKOFF: Instead of talking globally, I'm going to try and speak to some details. In Dr. Dewald's paper the issue of the therapist's neutrality is emphasized throughout, and the therapist's not gratifying the patient is also emphasized. It seems to me, in some conceptions of the therapeutic process, at least prospectively and in terms of studies of actual analyses of therapies, the therapists, even well trained therapists, appear to deviate from time to time and find themselves, at least retrospectively recognizing that they gratified patients, that they acted out with patients in one way or another. Not in a most gross way, but nevertheless these things occur and it seems to me that at least some analysts would describe the study of these kinds of interaction where there is a revivification of earlier role relationships by the therapist retrospectively with the patient, or by the therapist within himself, as often helpful in the change process. So, I will add that to what Dr. Dewald describes. Also, I would differ with his concept of acting out. It seems to me that during the course of a psychoanalysis, even in the later stages, not everything is combined to an understanding of the verbal messages or of the verbal statements that are made. Often information accrues from acting out that's not self-destructive or destructive to others or from various motor patterns that lead to insight and can be used

I think, at least if we get away from the earlier conception that acting out is instead of remembering and at least look at Ekstein's conception of acting out as being occasionally in the service of remembering, I would modify that definition that he applies to acting out.

Now, the other issue is in the termination phase. Do patients really give up the analyst? They certainly appear to. There is certainly an internalization of some of the analyst's functions and we think of that as part of the change and/or cure in psychoanalysis. But it also seems to us from other studies that when you interview people several years after a successful analysis, within the space of a couple of hours following another interviewer they get right back into the transference neurosis and it's repeated all over again. And the question then comes up, Are these people successfully analyzed? Were they successfully analyzed? To my way of thinking, there are many features of the transference neurosis. There are many conflicts that are understood and then the results and the capacities to understand these conflicts are internalized. But the potential for reexperiencing the same kinds of conflicts comes up in later life, whether it be in an altered form, or in one which can be quite readily understood. So, I would add that opinion to the concept of change. I don't think that the change goes so that a transference neurosis is completely resolved, at least to the extent that it doesn't reappear in other situations: nevertheless the potential is there.

To go on to Dr. Ornstein's paper, I'd like to just focus on the concept of empathy if I can, and wonder about the specifics of it. Namely, it seems to me that there are a whole host of situations in psychoanalytic psychotherapy, as well as in psychoanalysis, particularly with the more disturbed patients that we see, in which the vicissitudes of empathy are more complicated than are described. Namely, there are situations in which analysts very clearly have an understanding of the patient, and are able to impart this information to the patient, and the patient is able to know that the analyst understands him and empathizes with him. And this in turn is rejected by the patient for specific reasons that can turn on his development. For example, if an individual, who has a certain amount of narcissistic investment in analyzing himself, feels that the analyst is too close to understanding him, he can reject that understanding for that reason. Now, one could argue that true empathy would mean understanding that as well, and perhaps Dr. Ornstein would counter what I'm just criticizing about his concept of empathy with that remark. But I think there are a variety of situations in which empathy does not involve merely understanding. It involves the process of what it is that's going on between the patient and the analyst, and that often involves a great deal of frustration. It's often in moments of frustration where one understands one's frustration in relationship to what is going on with the patient — namely, signal affects that are evoked by the patient's particular resistance at that particular point, and how they might resolve or be connected with earlier difficulties that existed in the patient's life. This would strike me as being part of the vicissitudes of empathy. I find that the concept of the selfobject matrix is rather confusing. It seems to me that it is much more useful to consider that many of the conflicts that come up within the transference, for example, the issues of gratification or the failure to gratify within the transference and the therapeutic alliance have more to do with conflictual areas, and that the concept of selfobject is not nearly as explanatory as that of object. Even earlier, relationships don't fit in with the concept of just need, they fit in with conflict in my way of thinking. To illustrate that: a child may want to be fed but the whole issue of being fed or not being fed often involves a great deal of aggression. Just being fed, alone, may evoke guilt on the part of the child in that the child has aggressively grabbed something from the mother versus just having had his needs met. So it doesn't seem to be so simple as that needs are being fulfilled.

DR. LEON SALZMAN: These presentations that Dr. Michels has really formulated for us give us some opportunity to pursue what are the essential, crucial questions in this whole debate about whether psychotherapy is an inferior, lesser-depth form of therapy, and so forth. The description we have from Dr. Dewald is a beautiful description of what happens in a psychoanalytic process. I really ask you whether it even happens that way. It is beautiful in that it describes the ideal kind of formulation of how treatment should go and, in fact, in some idealized way Dr. Dewald talks about cure —

cure, not even with a question mark, or with a doubt or hesitation. I suspect that even the very title of this symposium should have had at least a question mark about cures. The description simply cannot come alive with regard to real patient and real activities. So I think it is a beautiful, idealized notion of how the therapeutic process goes, if you accept the classical psychoanalytic conceptions. This is the way I learned my psychoanalysis, way back in the institutes in 1940, when I graduated from a psychoanalytic institute. And it's almost sort of a revisit, because I don't see anything really changed in this formulation except that it's presented so beautifully, and so clearly, and, unfortunately from my point of view, as if it is a process that can be validated, can be experienced by others, can be reviewed in any way that would somehow give us a feeling of conviction about this description. So, I would ask Dr. Dewald to try, perhaps, to renew my faith in this kind of process, by asking him to tell us how often this happens and where is the analyst who can do it this well. Who? Where? It is a beautiful analyst who performs in the way described by Dr. Dewald.

Dr. Ornstein also renewed some of my past, because it seems to me that I'm hearing Dr. Harry Stack Sullivan right out of the grave. Beautifully presented in the language of self-psychology, the last revolution, if you live in psychoanalytic theory. Kohut has made some important contributions in that he has renewed a great deal of the psychoanalytic community by a formulation that brings us deep into the century, rather than back again to the nineteenth, where Dr. Freud worked. That contribution is the realization that there is an interpersonal self or selfobject matrix both internally and externally that constitutes the development of personality. And so many of the concepts could be translated in Harry Stack Sullivan's terms.

The emphasis on empathy has really revived one of the lectures that I attended way back when Sullivan was teaching at the psychoanalytic institute, where empathy was the key issue in the beginnings of the development of personality. It is the capacity for empathic interchange between mother and child that Sullivan considered to be the matrix of all later developments. And it is very interesting to me that as you hear Dr. Ornstein, of course in a slightly different way, I think using a newer language, he formulates this as what treatment is about.

I have no uneasiness in the descriptions, neither of Dr. Dewald nor Dr. Ornstein, about how treatment progresses and how people get well, because each is obviously the kind of therapist that they are describing who can be useful. I would only ask that the conceptual underpinning for the work that they do be explored. Whether, in fact, it is because of their notions about personality development or whether it is something else that Dr. Frank has alluded to or a number of other issues about which we are still very unclear why change occurs. But I think change does occur. I think we can document it as Dr. Frank has indicated. I think we can formulate some kind of scheme of how it gets done, but I'm not sure we need the very complex, complicated, mechanical, structural bases to explain it. But if we do, then I guess we all have to get down to the business of learning it. But I'm not so sure that change is based on our real understanding of the structural so that then we can pursue treatment to illuminate and to then assist in the utilization of that illumination in order to produce change.

DR. JERRY LEWIS: I was impressed that some of the processes described by both of my colleagues seemed to be parallel or iso-morphic, but the conceptual understandings of cure seem to be very different. A couple of questions that I hope each of them would address. First, one for Dr. Dewald, and that is if he could help me understand the level or the processes which mediate the curative impact of the regressive transference. Could he even give me some kind of metaphor for understanding whether that replaces, alters, blunts, blurs – or what it does – the earlier internalized experiences with parents? Secondly, for Dr. Dewald also, I'm interested in the appropriate interpersonal relationship between analyst and patient which he states very clearly is in the form of an early parent/child relationship and I would like to ask the question, 'Should the relationship between psychotherapist and patient, dealing as he so clearly articulated, with derivative conflicts rather than core conflicts, have that same structure? Should it be facilitated or should the patient/therapist real relationship be structured under optimum circumstances or evolve under optimum circumstances in a way that is not clearly parent/child?' For Dr. Ornstein, having some interest myself in the empathic process, in teaching it, insofar as one believes it can be taught, I need some help in clarifying the path of empathy between self and selfobject. I am struggling in my own mind, although I think I understand empathy as it is a process in therapy between therapist and patient, I need some clarification on that particular descriptive phrase or metaphor, the path of empathy between self and self-object on an adult mature level.

DR. MICHELS: Dr. Frank, as the senior psychoanalyst watcher on the panel —

DR. JEROME FRANK: I'm having great difficulty as you might expect. I haven't been near an institute since 1949 and I'm very much aware that I'm now an outsider. I have a mixture of great admiration and great frustration over these two papers. I admire them because they are beautifully constructed, consistent, elaborated, theoretical conceptualizations that explain a great many aspects about human nature, and about human functioning, and about therapy. But I don't know how to evaluate that. One way to evaluate, I suppose is the artistic one; does it make good sense? Well, Freud, you know, won a prize for literature, which I think was extremely well deserved. This is a convincing, attractive system which didn't make sense to you but seemed to illuminate reality. Well, both are. I can't judge on that basis at all. The other is the empirical one. Where does this touch ground? The kind of thing that Dr. Salzman was talking about. And here, again, one is in grave difficulty. What kind of empirical data could we use to support or test these? Although I'm not an analyst, and although I dropped out of the analytic institute, I was analyzed. I can't verify in myself any of these processes, really. It helped me a great deal but I can't relate it to this, and I'm reminded of the fact, of course, that from a research standpoint all the evidence says therapists do not do what they say they do, starting with Freud. Freud was apparently anything but that passive mirror he liked to claim should be required of the analyst. In some accounts he really was very active throughout the session. In others, he might have maintained that detachment during the session, but they say that he talked a blue streak with the patient between the couch and the door. That was coincident to therapy.

But that might be where it all happened. And, of course, he gave patients money and all that kind of thing.

I'm stuck. I can't really evaluate these two theories, these two systems. I have a couple of comments which again I offer with great diffidence because I can't relate them to any real data, but, to me, both are too much into framing the whole discussion in terms of intrapsychic change. The rest of the world is smuggled in, somehow, to the transference reaction. But the assumption seems to be that everything that's important is going on in therapy. Now, we know that even if you are being seen five times a week, that's less than 10 percent of the time that you are awake, and I can't believe that therapy is so important that nothing important is going on the *rest* of the time. And it may well be that that's how therapy works, primarily because it leaves the patient to behave differently during the rest of the week, which gives him a different kind of feedback. At a meeting just the other day, as a little example of this, there was a discussion on the therapy of agoraphobia. The therapist compared the results of treatment when he saw the patient alone, and when he saw the patient with his spouse. There were fourteen cases in each condition, and when the spouse was not included less than half improved – only six. When the spouse was included, 90 percent improved. Since people are interactive, open systems, any really satisfying theory would have to include the rest of the world.

Dr. Dewald greatly stressed effects of the regressive transference neurosis, which, of course, is highly emotionally charged, and as I mentioned this morning, that may really be a way in which therapy produces changes. But then the question comes up, If it is, can one produce a regressive transference neurosis in a much simpler shorter way? One way, of course, would be through drugs. A great deal of work has been done with LSD which describes cases in which, if you get to the right level of dosage, you have a psychoanalysis at that particular level and the infantile memory comes back with a great deal of emotional charge. If you feel that medications hopelessly complicate situations, which indeed they may, then you have things like implosion therapy, or est, or all of these, which try directly to produce what has been called a regressive transference neurosis. Perhaps it would work much more efficiently than the psychoanalytic model.

DR. PAUL DEWALD: These reactions have highlighted a number of issues. In response to Dr. Skolnikoff, I agree that many times there are elements in the psychoanalytic situation which are gratifying. Those ultimately, hopefully, will be analyzed. Sometimes they are inherent, namely a patient who likes to talk and be listened to, and that's part of the analytic process. But if, after a while, the response is, "Why don't you ever tell me how well I am doing and how much I'm telling you about myself?", then the therapist has an opportunity to analyze that gratification. As far as acting-out is concerned, yet, it is an intermediate form of communication from which one can derive a great deal of information. When it is ultimately subjected to verbal and interchanging analysis that takes the place of the behavior, then it can be gradually converted from behavior to thought and made an internal as well as a verbal interpersonal process. As far as the termination issues are concerned, I agree with Dr. Skolnikoff completely, that there is a continuing potential for development of transference. And I think I alluded to that in my paper when I said that the infantile and childhood impulses are never extinguished. The potential to reactivate them is there. The big difference is that, yes, a transference neurosis exists, but, yes, it is also quickly resolved, reintegrated, and the individual is capable of dipping into his primitive core and coming back out again without undue conflict and without a fixed regression.

Dr. Salzman's comments are difficult to address, because he and I obviously have had a very different experience. My own experience is not only my own but also that of the students whom I supervise and I can document from their work with their patients as it is reported to me that certain kinds of interventions seem to produce negative effects and other kinds of interventions seem to produce more salutary effects. Is there ever a perfect psychoanalysis? No. Is this a distillation of a variety of experiences from a variety of different patients? Yes. In the original paper* I have

---

*Dewald, P. A., "Elements of change and cure in psychoanalysis," *Archives of General Psychiatry* 1983, *40*, 89-95.

illustrations in a clinical form of the kinds of experiences that I am referring to, what the responses were, and how they were taking place. Dr. Salzman raises, for us, a very important methodological question about validation. How do we validate? This, I am afraid, is a methodological problem that I don't have the answers to. Some people are trying to work toward that aim in terms of, for example, tape recording. On the other hand there is no question that the introduction of the tape recording does alter the process to some extent. So that's a subject for the future.

Dr. Lewis asked about the immediate and curative impact of the regressive transference and what happens to the earlier influences? Again this is difficult to get across in just a few moments, but let me suggest, for example, that if the patient in the transference experience has a literal fantasy for you, the analyst, who are about to castrate him for his interest in his wife and for the fact that he has had sex with her the night before, and you are sharply disapproving, and then he recalls fantasies of what transpired in his multiple dreams as a child and so on, and gradually this internal psychological fantasy experience, *vis-à-vis* you, gets modified by his experience that, although he expects you to be angry – you are not, a previously pathogenic fantasy is now gradually being modified into, "I used to think that," or "I can remember, now, that when I was a kid thus and so, but now I can really feel and see that it wasn't so." The same is true vis-à-vis the patient, the derivative in the psychotherapy situation; and I would emphasize again, the analyst is not the parent. The patient who sees the analyst in a parental role has to ultimately renounce that as a wish. Here again is where the analytic experience provides, in the transference, a current, immediate living opportunity to do so. Again, in terms of Dr. Frank's comments, I think he sets up something of a strawman and then knocks it down very adeptly. Yes, there is an external world, and yes, the four or five hours a week that the patient spends with the analyst is only a tiny fraction of that which transpires in a patient's life. If any patient talks only about the intrapsychic process, if any patient talks only about reconstructions of earlier, and genetic, and infantile, and early childhood fantasies, if any patient talks only about the immediacy of the transference experience, I would say that this is manifestation of a major and significant resistance that needs to be analyzed. The analysis is isolated from the rest of the individual's life. Analysis is useless unless it relates to the patient's everyday, current, immediate life and all of the various influences in it. So I don't go along with that as a critique of this process. He's asking for empirical data. I would say the same thing to him, Yes, we do need empirical data. I can document this from my own experience only in the sense that these are clinical phenomena. Recording these, making the data available to some other interpretation, that's where the field as a whole is in a bad spot and I think we do have to make attempts to get that primary data somehow.

DR. PAUL ORNSTEIN: I would also do what Dr. Dewald did, select a few points I can briefly answer now, and hope to take up some of the other issues later. Starting with Dr. Michels' question regarding optimum frustration, is it just a little bit of frustration and how does one decide? This is an important question in psychoanalysis because many of the debates have gone around the issue, "Just what is abstinence? How far should it be maintained?" As far back as 1932 Michael Balint stated that, as he observed it, the psychoanalytic situation created what he called excessive frustration. As a result of the excessive frustration certain data emerged in the analysis which, according to him, were more artifacts of the excessive frustration than real remobilization of early childhood or infantile developmental issues, and, therefore, they led to false assumptions about development, and led to faulty psychoanalytic techniques. Nobody has picked it up since, systematically, but this statement impressed me way back, a long time ago. So when I studied Heinz Kohut and Phil Seitz' 1962 paper, in which both of them, but primarily Kohut, were extending what was then Hartmanian ego psychology, prior to Kohut's turning to the study of narcissism and the self, he made the following point in trying to pictorialize the mental apparatus, or the psyche. He called one side of the psyche the divided part, where the repression barrier was the result of what he termed excessive frustration. The other side of this divided psyche was what he called then progressive neutralization, where no repression barrier developed either from pressure from within or pressure from without, which the repression barrier was conceived of as responding to parental responses and frustrations, and he called the experiences that allowed for progressive transformation of archaic experience optimum frustration. Then, surveying the entire psychoanalytic literature, development, and so on, he concluded that psychoanalysts, by and large, always felt that it was optimum frustration that led to normal psychological development. So this is the initial point of view. Now, in the psychoanalytic process, based on self-psychology, as he reconstructed the early self — the self-object relation — he recognized that analysts had become phobic of gratifying patients because of the idea that drive needs leaked out, and if they leaked out, not enough energy would be available for the analysis of them in some ways. And that was sort of a funny concept, but that's how certain abstinence rules seemed to have been solidified, rather than based on what was optimally allowing the patient to feel the safety of the analytic or psychoanalytic situation and allowing him to let whatever had been repressed or disallowed to emerge for analysis. So the climate is something that the analyst creates for a purpose and that purpose still requires neutrality. But neutrality is not the absence of warmth, or genuine presence in the analytic situation, or any of that. It is only guarding against the intrusion of the analyst's presence, so as not to muddy the water. But it does not mean that one has to be there as if one wasn't there. That is the kind of situation that Balint referred to as creating the problems. So optimum frustration means an empathic perception of the patient's needs which never can be gratified. It can only be understood and explained. In other words, only understanding and interpretation can be offered, but that doesn't mean the analyst can be as he is, either warm or not so warm, distant or not so distant; his warmth or distance is part of what creates the transference picture and that has to be included in the interpretive activity.

Now what is empathy in its basic definition and mode of observation? In order to counter Dr. Salzman's suggestion that Sullivan already introduced it, I would say yes, to a certain degree he has and there is no need to argue about priority here or whether this is being revisited or not. What is definitely not part of the Sullivanian approach, although, as I say, some aspects are, is the early infantile mother/child relationship. The empathy there is all part of it. The analyst's need for empathy is part of it, although empathy may be a different process as defined by Sullivan and Kohut. Kohut made the following statement in 1969: "Empathy as a mode of observation defines the field." He said psychoanalysis is whatever aspect of reality can be encompassed with the empathic mode of observation. Now, here is where the complication arises, but we can't sidestep it. When a patient feels that we make the effort at seeing the world from his or her vantage point, that makes a tremendous impact on the patient and the patient's reaction to the analyst's simple observational mode of empathy is already enormous. This is in contrast to the analyst's maintaining an external observer's point of view, and insisting that he knows better what the patient's reality is, or should be, and then offering this corrective reality. The patient will turn to his own correcting of his own reality distortions if he feels, senses, and experiences that the analyst is in tune with his empathy. A patient of mine rather repeatedly, because I have my limits of empathy with him, tells me that I miss step one. Just yesterday, step one would have been for me to recognize that in the dreams, of which he presented three in a row, he portrayed how miserable he felt throughout the last two or three days because he was so deeply misunderstood by me that this suffering was creating a great deal of distance between us. I sensed that. I knew it. But I made no comments at that point about it because there was another aspect to all three dreams and as part of either countertransference, or whatever, I focused on the part that he was telling me, that in spite of how damaged he felt, he recovered. And I focused on that, whereupon he said, "You never seem to want to accept my suffering. You need to turn it into some kind of strengths. You don't understand me. And when you don't understand me like that, that means you don't accept my suffering self, all the agony I go through," etc. The important issue here is that he needs to be understood and while he agreed later on in the next session (He's from out of town; I see him twice a day. This was in the morning), in the afternoon, he agreed that I was, in my second step right. But he said, "If you go to step two, that means you're presenting your ideas and it's more important for you to make a point than for you to recognize and validate my self experience." I think this is one way to indicate the role and function of empathy. While my mode of observation may have been corrected, I was not empathic enough to know that, at that moment, what was most significant was the acknowledgment of his experience whereupon he would have, as he did in other occasions, said, "But, you know, in addition to that, I also think that the dream contains such and such." And it is, I think, on that basis that we need to study the impact of empathy on our patients. I would respond to the other comments in our next dialogue because I don't have any more time now.

DR. MICHELS: One of my questions for our next dialogue is to ask Dr. Dewald, first, and then Dr. Ornstein, whether that patient we just heard about, craving for empathic understanding was something fundamental to the nature of the therapeutic process or was the disguised transference wish that Ornstein failed to optimally frustrate?

7

Sharper Differences: Dialogue III

DR. ROBERT MICHELS: In June of 1882 Breuer stopped his treatment of Anna O, fled from it as a matter of fact, and in November of 1882, just over 100 years ago, he told Freud about the case and psychoanalysis began. From November, 1882 until 1897, for the first 15 years of the history of psychoanalysis, 15 percent of the total time, the basic model of psychoanalysis and of the genesis of psychopathology was that some traumatic event, rapidly recognized to be an event in the childhood of the patient, had caused the pathology and that the recovery of the memory of that event in the treatment was curative. The mechanism of cure was fairly clear at that time. Freud made a dramatic discovery in 1897. He discovered, as he reported to his correspondent friend Fliess, that his patients had been telling him things that weren't true and the traumatic events that they described to him and that he assumed were etiologic had often, if not generally, not occurred. They had simply been the results of the patients' imaginations.

A minor figure would have hoped that no one else found out the same thing. A great figure would have reported his error and retracted his theory. A genius like Freud did neither of those. He reported his error but maintained his theory, pointing out that this was an even more important discovery because it meant that the traumatic experiences which he had thought reflected something about the adult's behavior with children, in fact, told us something about the mind of the growing child, that the traumatic events of childhood which were pathogenic were really fantasies rather than events in the life of the child. It's in this second birth of psychoanalysis, in 1897, that modern psychoanalytic thinking begins. Or at least begins for me. And now starts my question, because central to that notion is that what was pathogenic for the child in psychoanalytic theory was not the way that he was treated by his parents, was not the way he was understood or misunderstood or traumatized, and that treating him well can't be curative because treating him badly was not the problem in the first place. Yes, it's true that our patients report that they were unloved and misunderstood and raised unempathically, but from 1897 until 1980 all psychoanalysts knew that those reports were based on fantasies of childhood which structured transference relationships and the transference was a clue to understanding the fantasy. Now, I was comfortable with that theory; I'd been taught it, I'd learned it, I taught it, and I used it. But now I'm confused because two distinguished psychoanalysts, Drs. Dewald and Ornstein, are shaking the very foundations of psychoanalytic theory by the papers they have given us. Dr. Dewald is suggesting that a critical element in the mechanism of action of psychoanalytic treatment is that the analyst behaves differently than the way the primary object behaved. But as I understood the theory there was nothing wrong with the way the primary object behaved. Dr. Ornstein tells me that a critical element in the theory of psychoanalytic change and cure is that the analyst, unlike the parent, is empathic. But I thought the complaint that the parent was unempathic was simply a fantasy that was being reconstructed in the transference rather than a veridical memory of an actual childhood trauma. Did I miss something? Was Freud wrong in 1897? I ask Drs. Dewald and Ornstein if they can reply to that.

DR. PAUL DEWALD: As usual, Dr. Michels puts his finger on the heart of an issue very cogently, directly, and clearly. I think the mistake is in trying to look at this from an either/or perspective. It is true that initially Freud did have the seduction theory as the etiology of neuroses by which the active seducer ended up as an obsessional and the passively seduced individual ended up as an hysteric. It's true about his early theories about catharsis and abreaction of repressed reminiscences. He then swung from that extreme to the opposite extreme. I think we are beginning now to recognize other possibilities. Just to illustrate, overt incest was originally thought to be the full etiological explanation. Then it was thought to be entirely fantasy, and now we have studies which demonstrate that probably 10 to 20 or 25 percent of children are sexually abused by either direct or symbolic incestuous experiences with adults. So, we are seeing the pendulum swing back. I think the mistake here is to think of it as an either/or proposition. I think that the childhood fantasies, and the child's primitive experience of reality, and the child's idiosyncratic and personalized interpretation of that reality colored by his own innate wishes, desires, needs, drives, fears, fantasies, defenses, and adaptive devices, layered in various developing structures, influence how the child perceives the real experiences around him. Vice versa, certain kinds of real experiences can activate in the child, or can reinforce in the child, or can oppose or strengthen in the child, a variety of intrapsychic fantasies. So, I do not see it as an either/or proposition any more than I see pathology as either a deficiency or a conflict but, rather, both. It seems to me that fixation is related to conflict and conflict can in turn invoke various levels of fixation. So it seems to me that your question really is one that we cannot answer other than in a general sense, except through the detailed understanding and analytic scrutiny in the individual case as we try to weigh which is which. Now, as far as the analyst's behaving differently than the original objects as an element in the treatment process, I presented and emphasized that aspect in my paper, largely because for many individuals it remains a rather vague kind of background taken for granted, while the real issues in analysis, or the curative factors, are to be found elsewhere. My point would be that the reliving of these infantile and early childhood developmental crises with a new object is only one of a large variety of factors that contribute to change in the process of analysis.

DR. PAUL ORNSTEIN: I also like the way Dr. Michels phrased the question because of its straightforwardness, directness, and because it allows me to join Dr. Dewald in offering an answer. I am only going to pick up where he left off by saying that rather than viewing this as an either/or proposition, he would now feel that both issues are present. Both issues are important − the unconscious childhood or infantile fantasy as well as the actual experiences that the child had at the hands of his or her primary objects. My problem with this "both," rather than "either/or," formulation is that I would like to know if, in a way, it is at all possible to know which one is primary. Is the fantasy primary as a pathogenic factor or are the experiences primary? Does the fantasy precede the experience, and perhaps become intensified as a result of it, or are fantasy and experience unrelated to each other as in Dr. Michels' formulation, and which the classical view seems to maintain. Maintaining the primacy of fantasy and, therefore, disregarding, to a rather great degree, at least in theory if not in practice, the experiences has to do with wanting to maintain the primacy of drives in relation to personal development.

Let me digress for one moment and give you an example. Kris made beautiful observations in relation to a particular child whose parents he knew. He was able in the reconstruction of the history and what was pathogenic for this child, to recognize the parental impact on the child's experiences as almost overriding. But then he asked the question, "What would happen if this person would go to an analyst 20 years later?" It would be the little girl's oedipal wish toward the father and the rejection of the mother, or the hate for the mother that would be reconstructed by the analyst as the significant pathogenic factors and yet he gave no absolute evidence for the fact that the mother could not tolerate the little girl's budding sexuality and closeness to the father and seductiveness or coyness vis-à-vis the father. So it was the mother, whose inability to tolerate what was a normal developmental phase in the little girl, seemed to Kris to have been the significant factor, but he had to disregard that because the theory required that he see it as being reconstructed from the vantage point of primary drives. Therefore, my answer to Bob Michels is that while I find myself on this panel closest to Paul Dewald in my basic orientation, although I have disagreement with some of the things that he has stated in his paper, indeed, times have changed. By going to the point of the empirical data in the observation of self-object transferences, we have the ability to see and observe without needing to speculate if we are willing to take these observations as the starting points for reconstructions. Our patients, indeed, react to our lack of empathy. The trauma that we might inadvertently or naturally, in the course of analysis, inflict on them is, indeed, traumatic to them, although we don't understand, because it reawakens their feelings on earlier issues in relation to their parental self-object. In other words, when I don't understand the patient in a particular way, it is traumatic to him or her because that is already the vulnerable point which the patient has carried along from early infancy or childhood. Seeing, therefore, in that context what is traumatic, one can make more reliable reconstructions about early development.

DR. ROBERT MICHELS: I want to point out the structure of Dr. Ornstein's argument and a parallel. He's saying that he's not arguing from theory; he's arguing from data, empirical clinical data. The data are that in the transference, when the patients' cravings for empathy are frustrated or gratified, they act in certain ways, showing that they were deprived of the needed nurturant empathy in their original development. I'm convinced by that, just as I was convinced by Freud between 1882 and 1897 when he used exactly the same argument to demonstrate the truth of the patient's reports of childhood sexual trauma. Their craving for sensual gratification in the transference relationship was authentic and deep and real and, whether it was gratified or frustrated, had a sharp impact on their behavior and on their development. Freud believed for fifteen years what Ornstein has believed for only two or three. How am I to know when Ornstein will see the light? But I can't give him a chance to answer that because Dr. Salzman wants to say something.

DR. LEON SALZMAN: Yes, I would like to comment on this very crucial issue, because I think it is neither/nor not an either/or. There is a serious question as to whether a reliving, a revivification, a review of the infantile situation or the earlier developmental situation is at all necessary for what we are here to discuss, which is cures, changes in the overt behavior and in the psychic behavior of our patients. Now this is a very serious question. At the point of Freud's dilemma, when he discovered that his patients who talked about being sexually assaulted were describing fantasies, he changed radically his whole theory of obsessional states. Freud's genius at that time was to take a factual, evident, observed phenomenon and to change it into the true, ultimate value of the whole psycho-dynamic psychoanalytic discipline – the discovery that what a person thinks has happened to him, not what has actually happened to him, is the crucial issue. So, what are we reliving? There is no point, from one framework, of talking about a reconstruction and a review and a need to revive what was a conception of an infant's experience, which in the developmental process began to have and make an impact on the way he dealt with his subsequent living. Now that's what we have to face when our 20-year-old, 13-year-old or 50-year-old patient comes to our office. They are now acting, living, performing in a way that certainly had a historical develop-mental basis. This is clearly so, but what we have to deal with is what they are doing today, and the only way we can understand how they have come to be what they are is to understand what they are doing today. Now, there is no doubt in my mind that if you can actually reconstruct, you will get some conviction about the development in that process. If you can actually go back, if your memory is capable of truly reviving how you did experience relationships at two or three or one, we would have very convincing documentation of not only our theory but of the therapeutic pro-cess. But, in fact, most of our patients can and do make major changes in their living without any necessity for reexperiencing that infantile process. They only need to recognize that, in fact, that process existed, that the process perhaps influenced their ways of looking at themselves and others. Perhaps that process has a major effect on their self, developmental self, object self-system. (The whole lingo that we have gotten caught up in that seems to me to be very confusing, but perhaps it's important – some structural understanding.) But I like to stay with the clinical. I hope the future of psychodynamic theory will go not in the direction of the arguments of the Kohutians and Kernbergians but in the direction of the application of our theory to treatment, particularly to answer whether in a clinical sense we actually need a revivification for there to be significant change. My answer, and my own experience, is that it is probably not necessary. On the other hand, I have certainly been impressed with the fact that if you can get it, you have a tool that is extremely effective in producing and in maintaining change in your patients. So, I think Freud was right in the first place when he thought it was trauma. He was right in the second place when he discovered it was not trauma. And he's right to this very day, except that our convoluted expositions of Freud's theory have gotten us way off from where Freud was. I think it is perfectly true to say that Freud was not a Freudian therapist at all. If anything, he was a most wild therapist in our terms, today. But Freud was the most psychodynamic theorist that the world has yet discovered.

DR. JEROME FRANK: First I want to say that I agree with Dr. Salzman that one doesn't have to go into the past to change the present. I really want to introduce another note of doubt or caution into all of this, a very fundamental one, and that's the validity of the evidential base on which all psychoanalytic theory rests. It rests on patient's reports to the analyst about what happened. Now, Freud thought that his method would yield objective data, because the analyst is simply a mirror and the patient is allowed to freely associate without being influenced by the analyst. By now it is perfectly clear that this is an extremely powerful influencing situation. In fact, it is very analogous to one of the most successful forms of brainwashing, that is, the prisoner is asked to confess, but he is never told whether his confession is right or not. He is just told to keep on confessing and eventually something good will happen. This is what you really have in an analytic situation –

where the patient comes to the analyst because he is in distress. He's like a prisoner in that sense. He's looking to the analyst for relief and the analyst doesn't give him relief, he just says, go on talking, go on free associating and eventually you will get relief. But this creates a situation that I remember when I was in analysis, where the analysand becomes extremely sensitive to the slightest cues to what interests the analyst and what doesn't. I remember seeing the analyst's foot waving out of the corner of my eye, noting when he seemed to be writing; things like this. All the time the analyst is subtly guiding what the analysand comes up with. The essential point is that this can lead to false memory. This was shown in brainwashing. Very often the prisoner would finally confess to things he really thought had happened which had never happened. So, I would raise the question about the whole basis for our theories here.

DR. PAUL DEWALD: To speak first to Dr. Salzman's point, I agree with him completely. When we talk about psychoanalysis we are talking about two or maybe three different things, and this, I think, needs to be reiterated. On the one hand, we are talking about a method of observation. Dr. Frank has just said that there are elements of suggestion in the analytic process; no question about that. If you stay silent for twenty minutes and you say to the patient, "Tell me something more about that," that becomes a very powerful suggestion. I agree with him completely. But the analyst doing this has to be aware of the power of his or her suggestive position, has to recognize the need for and attempt, at least, to maintain some sort of balance to recognize when he or she is trying to motivate or inform or instruct. The analyst has to recognize the temptation in the countertransference to feel that he knows what the patient really thinks and to tell the patient. Rather, the analyst must set the stage to permit the patient to increasingly become aware within himself. Whether things are real or unreal, again I'll go back to Dr. Frank's earlier position, the assumptive perspective about what the meanings of certain events, experiences, fantasies, relationships are, is determined by a variety of internal factors including drive and wish elements, including perceptions of the reality at the time, including intrapsychic fantasies which are the combined result or which can be perceived as the final result of the variety of different impinging forces organized simultaneously, analogous as Arlow has pointed out, to the use of myth. So all of this may be a personal myth of the individual, but it is a coherent thing which, once understood, gives us a line of understanding of how the mind works. But that's not a therapeutic application, it's a method of observation.

Secondly, it can be a method of therapy, and for certain individuals, maybe 5 percent, maybe 10 percent of the population at the most, is the treatment of choice. For the vast number of other individuals it is not. It may be contraindicated. It may make people worse. It may or may not necessarily make them any better. The place where analysis is going to live or die is the place where dynamic theory is helpful. The place where Freud himself indicated analysis is, has a contribution to make, is in a theory of the mind and in the understanding of human behavior which includes the whole gamut of the psychotherapeutic. Whether we are talking about supportive or uncovering whether we are talking about group or individual, whether we are talking about stated or unstated, whether we are talking about Weightwatchers and Alcoholics Anonymous, or est, or TA, or any of these therapeutic modalities, one can look at them from an analytic perspective and begin, then, from a clinical, theoretical position to understand how and why they work, and hopefully improve our techniques in doing so.

DR. MICHELS: We are talking about several things at one time. The original one, I think, involves a term that no one has mentioned but is hovering around here. It is psychic reality and the relationship of material reality to psychic reality. This is something that bothered Freud throughout his writing and continues to be of interest to analysts. I want to broaden this a little bit to take in social reality, a special form of material reality, with a question to Dr. Lewis. What was the new marital adaptation of Mr. and Mrs. A. at the expense of the middle-aged son's depression? Did he have to take on the added burden of the parents' pathologic projections, which they no longer put on to each other, but which are still alive in them intrapsychically, that is, no real change? Another question grows out of the same query. If I understood his case yesterday, he suggested that the change in Mr. A., which occurred as a result of his fairly directive therapeutic intervention in the marital situation, permitted the occurrence of and the stabilization of an intrapsychic change in Mrs. A., which led to improvement. A naive psychoanalyst might be somewhat confused by this, suggesting that since the real objects that stabilize internal psychic structures are inner objects, objects that are defined as much by transference fantasies that are projected onto the outer world as by the reality of the individuals out there, a change in Mr. A. that made him discordant with Mrs. A.'s sadomasochistic fantasies, which she brought with her from her primary objects, should have simply led her to rev up the power of that transference fantasy and ignore the new Mr. A. or to obliterate him by insisting that he change back, or find some new object, or in some way or other reveal what we all know, which is the power of the neurotic past as such, so that manipulative changes in real people in the present do not make that much difference. I think it is the same question here, one version is, Did it just get projected elsewhere? and the other, Why didn't it get projected somewhere?

DR. JERRY LEWIS: I'm aware of the theoretical stands that indicate that if someone has been accepting a primitive projection and for some reason that person leaves, refuses to etc., etc., etc., the theoretical prediction is that the projector will find another object to project to, will have an increase in symptomatology, etc. All I can say about that is that it is an interesting theory. My experience does not confirm it. I'm sure that happens in some situations but I'm equally sure that it does not happen in other situations. As to the question about the middle-aged son's depression, I can only say this — we are well aware of the fact that any of us here, who has dealt extensively throughout our careers with adolescents and families, know something about family projection systems and the misuse of adolescent children or of younger children as recipients of projections from parents, and about the role of that process in the adolescent symptomatology. Now, whether or not the same things occur in a 40-year-old son who is no longer living at home, who is living 2,000 miles away, and whether or not what happened was as a result of Mrs. A. redirecting her projections to her 40-year-old son is a reasonable question. I happen to feel that it is clinically unlikely because I don't think the son continues to be in the social field and hasn't been for many years. Those are the kinds of things that I think we need to address in attempting to understand bridges between intrapsychic functioning and constructs and interpersonal functioning and constructs. I would make just one other comment about the remarks from the others of this group and share with you some interesting experiences which do not reflect rigorous data. We use a lot of videotapes and have a reasonable library of psychotherapy films from famous therapists. One of the interesting experiences is to watch, without the sound, the psychotherapeutic interaction and predict what the thematic aspects are from the verbal/ nonverbal postures, etc. The issue of how much of what gets talked about in psychotherapy reflects the agenda from the past and how much of it is subtly influenced by the moment to moment interaction between therapist and patient is a critical issue which we should not think of in either/or terms, but I invite you, sometimes, to watch (for 15 or 20 minutes) a psychotherapy film or session that you know nothing about, and watch the interaction and predict, if you will, what are the themes that they are talking about. What is the content: And I'm going to say that you often miss, but it is my impression, without rigorous design, etc., that an amazing number of times you can correctly presume the content of the exploration from your inferences about the nature of the doctor/ patient relationship based on posture and nonverbal communication and things like that.

DR. SALZMAN: Dr. Michels, I would like to raise the issue of projection and ask whether you assume or presume that there must be some place that it gets projected on when it is taken away from this place; whether Dr. Lewis doesn't look at projection in an unfortunately mechanical fashion? Now our theory somehow talks about it being projected onto an object and it's removed from the object and there it is lying loose and needs to be projected elsewhere. Can't we think of this phenomenon as something that occurs wholly inside that individual, that is, nothing is pushed out, nothing comes back, but it's an elaborate invention about how others think of me in terms of how I think of myself, etc., so that we won't need to find some alternative place for it to go.

DR. MICHELS: The answer is "sure" to the question that is phrased. I think it only is a psychological phenomenon, but I'm worrying about something that sounds a little like this. Paul Dewald said before, we have a treatment here that's good for 5 to 10 percent of people. My own view is that it's a generous estimate. Most of life's problems and most of destiny's tragedies are not treatable by psychotherapy, that's sad, but true. The domain where psychotherapy is effective is that small domain of human pain in which the cause of the pain has to do with the symbolic and fantasy elaborations of the individual that restructured the world, not to the real sources of pain in the material world. That's sad. It makes us weaker than we otherwise would be, but it's true. I think Jerry Frank made that point in his comments yesterday. Now for the 5 percent of people out there where important sources of pain are their symbolic elaborations of the material world, our exploration of their symbolic system can be critically important. Curative, I would even say. But we begin to get grandiose when we think, by exploring their symbolic world, we can undo real traumas. We can only treat fantasies. We can't treat realities. And what I'm prodding Paul Ornstein about is that he is, by manipulating fantasies, undoing the sequela of real trauma in early life. What I'm prodding Jerry Lewis about is that by manipulating contemporary reality he is trying to treat lifelong fantasy distortion without the direct exploration of those fantasies. They are both. Everyone is chiding me, saying, Bob, you are doing a wonderful job of articulating the theory and its a fascinating theory, but theory only goes so far and I've treated patients and patients are richer and more complex and more detailed and more sensitive than theory and let me tell you about what happens with real patients. And I'm glad that they are saying that because if they weren't, I would have to. And my job is easier because they are saying it first.

DR. ORNSTEIN: One thing needs to be responded to here, because it makes me nervous. I do not agree with any of you who would want to restrict the applicability of psychoanalytic understanding. I know you talked about psychoanalytic treatment and I certainly know that that is restricted, but I would not want to accept the statement that psychoanalytic treatment is appropriate only when there is a symbolic elaboration. I feel that now we have beginning evidence, not yet such that either Dr. Frank or Dr. Salzman or perhaps Dr. Lewis would immediately accept, but, nevertheless, growing clinical evidence that psychoanalysts rely on and then sometimes painfully give up when new evidence emerges, and I agree with Bob that maybe five years from now I will have different views and I will be very much ashamed about some of the ones that I will then consider to have been stupid at this time. But right now I am not ashamed and the view that I want to propose – that I'm rather, at the moment, enthusiastically convinced about – is that what I call arrest and structural deficiencies can, indeed, through the psychotherapy that is guided by contemporary psychoanalytic principles, be healed, whatever healing is. And here I want to tell you that most analysts, perhaps with the exception of Brenner and those who are close to him, including Anna Freud, believed that there are such things as developmental arrests. She made the statement that children who suffer from developmental arrest cannot be analyzed, that their reality has to be revamped and redone in order for them to be able to function better. Her dichotomy and other people's dichotomy in terms of arrest versus conflict is passé since Kohut introduced self-psychology and since Dewald is willing to include into his intrapsychic consideration that horrible word for classic analysts called "interpersonal." Later, I'll come back to the concept of the self-object, especially when I will respond to Dr. Salzman later on, how the concept of self-object serves us as a better clinical and psychoanalytic bridge between outside and inside that specious dichotomy, and how we can view anything from the inside if we can view it through that concept. So my main point in relation to Dr. Michels is that conflicts and arrests can be treated. Psychoanalysis is more applicable now than it ever was to the variety of psychological ills that we are confronted with.

DR. MICHELS: Now three questions which touch on similar more clinical things. (1) Why are all the panelists so defensive about the use of the term "corrective emotional experience," when, clearly, something like this must happen for a cure? (2) The second question is directed to Dr. Dewald: You didn't comment on Lewis' request for you to distinguish between the working of the therapeutic regression and the discredited corrective emotional experience. Will you comment? (3) The third question is aimed at Dr. Ornstein. What do you think about the observation that at moments of empathic failure intention, understanding, and change seem to occur? I want to ask Dr. Skolnikoff to start.

DR. ALAN SKOLNIKOFF: The term corrective emotional experience, I think, is misunderstood by many of us. By it I understand that the analyst or therapist makes a conscious decision, fairly early on in the treatment, to act in such a way to repair the difficulties that the patient had with the original objects, the traumatic experiences or the traumatic relationship that the patient had with the original object. By that, he consciously develops the relationship or acts in such a way as to repair that poor experience. The reason why I think that that's such a poor thing to do is that we don't know — if we're engaged with a patient in an attempt to discover what it is that happened to them, early on, and even in the middle and toward the end — we don't know all of the details of what they experienced as being traumatic in their original relationship with the object. Therefore, I artificially predetermine how I'm going to act, I'm essentially distorting and doing the sort of thing we've been talking about or that we've been arguing about, namely, we're assuming that such and such a thing happened where we really don't know that that happened, and we're acting in such a way to correct something that happened, when we don't understand what happened. What's corrective in the therapeutic experience, in my opinion, is the therapist and the patient attempting to find out what their version was about, what happened, and what's happening now. It's an attempt to look at the interaction between patient and therapist, both in the therapeutic alliance and in the transference, and to define what it is that's being experienced. In some therapies, the therapist describes what he is feeling with the patient. In most therapies, with the higher level disorders, one focuses on what the patient is feeling with respect to a variety of feelings that are coming up. Now, to answer Dr. Frank's statement from before, it seems to me that if in your analysis or other analyses of this kind, the analyst is unable to look at what the patient is doing to please the analyst, if the analyst is unaware of all of the subtle ways in which the patient is doing the variety of things to please him, that does not constitute a good analysis or a good therapeutic experience. The subtlety of the work in the transference, in the therapeutic alliance is to see and to follow each of these themes, namely the subtle ways in which the patient complies with the analyst's wishes and the subtle ways in which the patient defies what he thinks the analyst wants as reflected in the here and now transference. There are three elements: the past, the here and now, and the present. These are all intertwined. We always attempt to intertwine these and to understand all of these together. I just want to make one statement about Spence's essays on historical truth and narrative truth because they speak to the issue of what it is that we are doing. There is always the argument – are we reconstructing a narrative that is in the mind of the patient or in our minds – as to what it is that happened in their life? Or, are we reconstructing a historical truth? The argument I think is an interesting one and there is a lot of discussion about it. But as many of you know, about history – and I'm talking from the historical point of view outside of psychoanalysis – history has always been rewritten in history books depending on who wins the battle. It seems to me that we try to get to historical truth. We try eventually to find out what is real. But we probably are dealing with psychic reality at most times, even at the end, at the termination of the treatment.

DR. ORNSTEIN: My feeling is that a lot less misunderstanding would occur if we acknowledged, just on the basis of what several people have said and written, that we are not reconstructing actual reality. Freud was often confused about that. If you remember in *Moses and Monotheism*, for instance, when even he tried to apply reconstruction to historical truth, he came up with the idea that Moses was an Egyptian. Based on his kind of reconstruction, historians disputed that. What we are after in psychoanalysis is the experienced reality, not the actual reality. That is, not what the parents actually did, but how did the child experience it. As far as that goes, it is extremely important in the treatment process, no matter what Dr. Salzman experiences and what he says, to reconstruct that experienced reality because that is something the child felt then and the adult feels now. He is also right when he says we have to deal with what the patient brings now. But that now is a continuation of what was then, in terms of inner experience.

As far as corrective emotional experience goes, it got into ill repute because Alexander proposed that one should behave in an opposite way from the father. For instance, if the father was stern, one should be, let's say, fair; and if he were, let's say, fair, then one should be a little more strict. Those are rather manipulative ways. Corrective emotional experience is the important idea. That someone going through analysis, by whatever means, ultimately has to have a corrective experience as a sine qua non; if he doesn't have one, maybe he shouldn't pay his fees. I think Dr. Dewald made it clear in his paper that an analyst never uses this concept, but always banks on its being present because he says the distortions in the transference have to be corrected. How can you correct them if you behave exactly like the parents did? Against what will that correction occur? I don't happen to subscribe to the idea that to correct distortions is a primary task of the analyst. I feel that distortions get corrected if the analyst correctly understands what the patient is preoccupied with and is experiencing now and what the patient experienced then. In that sense, corrective emotional experience is part of every good treatment if the outcome is okay.

Now, the answer to the question regarding moments of empathic failure when change occurs, I think, is very much in tune with what I said before, about optimum frustration. I was citing Kohut from his preself-psychological stage of analytic development and Holt's self-psychological one; it is optimum frustration that stirs development in addition to the innate developmental tendency. Therefore, very frequently the trauma is minor, but it stirs the patient for further development. However, if you only have misunderstandings throughout the analysis, minor as they might be, and do not have long stretches of empathic contact and correct understanding, then these minor traumas will add up to a traumatic analysis which will not create change.

DR. MICHELS: I want to alert the audience to something that sounds like the panelists are arguing at each other, but I think they are agreeing. If I might paraphrase, Dr. Salzman is saying that treatment is about the present, fundamentally, centrally. And Dr. Lewis, I think, emphasized the same thing and Dr. Frank is insistent on that point. Change occurs by exploring the present. Dr. Ornstein and Dr. Dewald both say that it is terribly important to reconstruct a past. We can argue about whether it is a historical past or a psychic past – but a past. Those are not contradictory statements to me. Those apparently contradictory statements are totally compatible with each other because, I believe, for Dr. Ornstein and Dr. Dewald, the past they are talking about is a part of the psychic present and it is only insofar as it's part of the present that it is of interest to us and we are interested in reconstructing it. As analysts/psychotherapists, we are totally disinterested in that part of the past which is not also currently an active part of the patient's mental life. It is only the currently active fantasies which have their origins and may be cast in terms of the past that are of interest to psychoanalysis and psychotherapy. In fact, without exploring those it is impossible to thoroughly explore the present and there is no incompatibility with those positions. There is a trick meaning in psychoanalysis of the word "past" that one has to become familiar with.

DR. DEWALD: To just add one other point, it is very important to construct the past as it exists in the present in a psychoanalysis, in psychoanalytic psychotherapy to a somewhat lesser extent, in some aspects of supportive therapy even less than that. In other words, my point would be in the classical analytic technique and in the classical analytic situation, this becomes more important. Let me give a clinical vignette which I think is perhaps telling and could perhaps focus on what we are trying to say here. A psychiatrist analysand of mine, who has been in analysis for a very very severe phobic and anxiety state for some time, was preparing to take his American Board of Psychiatry examination. We discussed this in terms of what it meant to him, his current reaction to it, his fears, his fantasies of failure, etc. The day came when he went to take his exam and I terminated the hour in my usual way and he left. He came back, indicated how badly he had done. He knew at the time that he was doing very very badly. He knew what he should have done but didn't. He dismissed his patient after ten minutes having been told to keep the patient for at least ½ hour and he knew he failed, and sure enough he had. We discussed what this all meant.

It turned out that my not saying good luck when he left that last session meant to him I wanted him to fail, that I would be angry, challenged, competitive, resentful, bitter, castrate him if he dared to succeed. We worked this over. About six months later he went back to take the exam the second time. The same things happened, the activation of the conflict, the concerns, the questions, the doubts, and so on. He went, he comes back and reports he really did very well. He's quite convinced that he passed. He feels satisfied with his performance. About ten days later he gets the notification that he had passed and it's official. He comes in and tells me about it and we go on analyzing as usual. The next day he comes in and says there has been a terrible mistake; he feels he didn't pass after all. There has been a mistake in the computer and they are going to send him a notice tomorrow that he failed — why, because I didn't say "congratulations." This meant, again, he is threatened by castration because I didn't congratulate him, implying that my not offering him the congratulations meant I was angry, was threatened, was going to castrate him, etc. Now, in an analysis where I want to activate and deal with these kinds of intrapsychic transference phenomena, I maintain the situation of abstinence, which then tends to activate this kind of fantasy. In a less intensive psychotherapy one might very readily and humanly have said "good luck" and dealt with the patient's response to that comment. In a supportive psychotherapy one would have made a point of saying "good luck" and "congratulations, that's great." What I'm trying to point out, here, is that one uses these interactions and this kind of experience for one's strategic goals in treatment. And so that coming back, now, to the question of the corrective emotional experience and my position of reliving developmental crises, he was reliving a developmental crisis with me in which now, by his own experience, he would see that this idea that I didn't want him to pass came strictly from within him. I really didn't say anything about it and never gave him the indication that I didn't want him to pass. Now, he could see how he expected that from me. So that this, then, becomes a current situation and it was typical of his behavior in most current situations with various authority figures. We dealt with it at that level and in the reconstruction. Now, the point I'm trying to make is "yes, there is a corrective emotional experience" and I don't see that as a dirty word. The only way I see it as a difficult situation is the way in which Alexander prescribed it and used it, and the idea of manipulation. My point has been, if the analyst maintains an analytic posture where it continues to evoke or attempt understanding but does not respond in an active, manipulative, directive-modifying treatment way, then this kind of experience does occur.

DR. MICHELS: I think we are going to get some technical dissents on the management of that case. Dr. Salzman would you do it that way?

DR. SALZMAN: No I wouldn't. But before I get to a discussion of that very beautiful example that Dr. Dewald has given us, let me give you a little history about the corrective emotional experience. The problem was that Alexander, when he formulated this very interesting concept, thought that he knew what went wrong with that person. His theoretical background had convinced him. Alexander thought he knew what had caused the present problem, and that he could, through manipulative processes, undo it. A great idea, beautiful idea, only it doesn't work because he didn't know, and we don't know to this day, what are the actual elements. Because, if we did know them, I think it would be perfectly reasonable and fair to use our theory and apply it in a clinical sense. If, in fact, anger expressed inward is a cause of depression, and if we could allow the anger to be expressed outward, we should relieve depression. Well, unfortunately it doesn't do that. It doesn't work. Our theory somehow has to be much more sophisticated than that simple kind of formulation. So, the corrective emotional experience is not a bad phrase, not a bad word. As Dr. Ornstein and Dr. Dewald have pointed out, that's what we try to do all the time. But we are not quite so comfortable with our notion of what is specific. And that's where I think the case of Dr. Dewald would come right out with a neon sign. Dr. Dewald believes that by frustrating, by withholding, by a failure to be a human interactor and say "good luck," and "congratulations," he is expanding the patient's capacity to relive and, therefore, ultimately undoing what had been a previously bad experience. Now, if in fact that's true, then Dr. Dewald has been very effective in advancing the transferential neurotic inter-action so that the actual experience in the early years of a competi-tive parent or whatever the particular issues were, can be highlighted in a very dramatic way. And that is the purpose of the old trans-ferential issue — to highlight, to spotlight the early development of the present way of experiencing and functioning. But the whole question again is whether that is so. And whether this patient could not benefit from not having flunked that Board twice. If Dr. Dewald had clarified that in a continuous dialogue as to what this psychia-trist was experiencing, what he was expecting, then alternative ways of dealing with it are just as valid.

DR. ORNSTEIN: Now, while I said to you earlier that I felt on this panel closest to Dr. Dewald's view of things and his presentation, when he gave this example I felt very uneasy, because I couldn't easily tell the difference between Alexander and Dewald. The reason for my uneasiness and not being able to tell the difference is simply this. I would have behaved vis-á-vis this psychiatrist, whether he would be in supportive therapy, in intensive psychotherapy, or psychoanalysis, exactly the same way as far as my behavior is con-cerned. I have the feeling that if you decide that you don't do certain things, omit an ordinary "good luck" or whatever, that in itself creates a problem and the question then for me is this: Is what Dewald then sees as a reaction a revival of something from childhood, or has that been created by the absence of something in the present that should have been there? I have learned how to dare to say "good luck" to my patients, because, even though I trained in Chicago, I was trained not to say that. Nor to say "have a good vacation." But I overcame that the day after I graduated, and, therefore, I would say that it doesn't matter to me what kind of psychotherapy or psychoanalysis the patient is in, certain basic attitudes I have will come across, and then I will analyze their impact. I do not withhold these ordinary expressions because it seems to me that I get what Balint called, in 1932, artifacts of reconstruction.

DR. MICHELS: We have to stop this dialogue.

8

Change and the Therapeutic Process

Leon Salzman

To produce change in the psychotherapeutic process it is necessary to develop an understanding of how one came to behave as one does – called insight – as well as to have a firm commitment to change, which involves the issues of relationship, trust, and identification with the therapeutic agent. Whether this is charisma or a rational regard for the authority, it is an essential ingredient in the ultimate process, including suggestion, exhortation, or authoritative pressures.

In my opinion, the enlightenment process needs major clarification with regard to the concepts of psychic determinism, free association, and an interpretation of disputed and questionable theory. The commitment to change requires active, willful, determined and conscious decision, supported by the empathic therapist. This paper will discuss these issues. I will deal only with several matters that, in my opinion, seriously impair our ability to change the behavior of our patients. There are mutually agreed upon concepts and hypotheses that I will not review in this brief presentation. Space does not permit me to examine some of the more recent theoretical contributions of the ego and self theorists at this time, with their speculative descriptions of psychic development. In my review of the matter of psychic determinism and free will, I want to suggest how these concepts have prevented the therapeutic process from calling on the capacity for willful intention to initiate and sustain personality and behavioral changes.

What produces change through the psychotherapeutic process? There is undisputed evidence that behavior change can occur through the influence of drugs, conditioning, or organic disease processes in the brain. How do the cognitive, linguistic, nonverbal communicative processes effect change? Evidence of such a possibility can be dramatically demonstrated in religious and other mystical encounters when conversion or other massive changes occur. In voodoo deaths, the "word" can produce lethal adrenal insufficiency, and forgiveness from the chief produces an immediate and striking change in the dying person. These instances provide major clues to the destructiveness of a psychic trauma and efficacious potential of a communicated feeling.

Theories of change are determined by prevailing concepts of disease. Time does not permit a review of the shift from the theological-invasive concept to the physiological-organic and presently, the psychological-developmental concept of mental illness. However, these phases may be summarized by describing three varieties of healers:

1. The wise, magical healer relationship in which the healer is possessed of spiritual values and wisdom and is able to alter the behavior of individuals in striking ways. The patient is required to accept the authority whether it be a physician, psychoanalyst, or priest, with faith and spiritual conviction;

2. the skilled, detached scientist who is uninvolved and may even be ruthless although somewhat less grandiose because

he recognizes his limitations and his responsibilities. He functions as a specialist who uses techniques that do not depend entirely upon his charisma and magical qualities; and

3. the expert-partnership relationship, in which the helper is a supportive, understanding person who guides and encourages with his knowledge and understanding and enables the patient to grow through his own understanding.

These three models relate to the spiritual-charismatic and authoritarian therapies based largely on faith and those which attempt to educate the individual to mental health. The categories are related to our knowledge and understanding of disease processes and determine the character of health delivery systems. Consequently, our capacity to heal influences the disorders that require healing.

It is the last two types of healing I propose to focus on and mainly on the philosophy of mental illness as it influences our views of change instead of discussing "cures," which is a loaded term in psychiatry.

It has only been in the last century that human behavior has been viewed as a complex integration of basic biological needs and essential cultural adaptations. Previously, man was seen as having animal needs and a spiritual nature endowed by God, which gave him the capacity to choose right from wrong and good from evil. Developments in science, especially the theory of evolution, supplanted the theological conception. The biological instinct hypothesis deemphasized man's freedom of choice and action and attributed most of his behavior to preformed, naturalistic, unchangeable and instinctual forces. Paradoxically, this view postulated a mind-body dichotomy which assumed that a person could, if he wished, alter his behavior but yet he was constrained by his biology. In the late nineteenth century Freud's discoveries enabled us to see that irrational, discrepant, or ego-alien behavior was not due to possession or invasion by demonic forces. Nevertheless, it is still widely believed that distorted behavior is deliberately conceived, stubbornly and wittingly maintained, and can be terminated by volitional means.

First, we can look upon some of the concepts that constitute the essential pillars of our mutually agreed upon psychodynamic theories of behavior. There are several that seriously limit our ability to limit our patient's behavior. They are not structural theories or developmental concepts but basic philosophical issues that underlie our understanding and interpretations to our patients.

The concept of psychic determinism and the wish-fulfilling hypothesis reinforce the idea that a person behaves the way he or she does by choice. For example, if a person is annoying or irritating, it must be because he wishes to alienate or antagonize others, and therefore his behavior reflects this wish. He may have some deep need to be rejected or some masochistic wish to be humiliated, which is ultimately related to his death instinct. Consequently, his behavior, though seemingly contradictory and irrational, is consistent with his unconscious desires according to classical psychoanalytic theory. In the motivational description of behavior, it is assumed that the consequences of the behavior are just what the person intended and designed.

Without abandoning any portion of the concept of the unconscious, one may view the consequences of behavior in a different framework; taking into account the patient's intent and also examining the state of mind, expectations, and needs of the recipient of the behavior. This approach reflects the interactional view of human behavior; it acknowledges that he may be annoying to others not because he wishes to irritate or antagonize but because of the manner in which he attempts to form a relationship. The need for acceptance may be so intense that one becomes overly aggressive and persistent, thus irritating and annoying the other person and causing the very opposite effect that one intends. The person who is annoying, irritating, or hostile may be so because he is trying too hard to be pleasing and accepted, and overdoes it by excessive behavior. Instead of a deep unconscious need to be rejected, he has an exaggerated need for acceptance because of his underlying feelings of worthlessness. His behavior is not wish-fulfilling because the anxiety involved in his neurotic needs promotes a failure in his performance. His anxiety alters his behavior rather than the effect produced by some deep underlying wish or need. Both this view and the wish-fulfilling hypothesis support the concept of an unconscious or state of unawareness. It does not deny the unconscious. One view under-lines the role of anxiety in distorting efforts made to fulfill one's needs and the other maintains that one's overt behavior is always a clear statement of one's unconscious wishes. This is an essential issue in the philosophy and technique of therapy so that all the formulations previously described are clearly related to whether this is a valid distinction I am raising. We can direct our attention to discovering what the unconscious really wants us to do or we can explore the behavior in terms of its intent and its effects. Thus we can have an interpersonal, interactional model of human behavior or an intrapersonal, instinctual model. Mostly we have both because many therapists are unclear as to which model they are using.

Freud covertly supported the concept of willfulness and choice in human behavior when he pointed out that the dominating goals of behavior are the pursuit of pleasure and the avoidance of pain, except in cases where realistic requirements demand some modification. Yet in his discovery and illumination of the uncon-scious and his attribution of instincts in human activity he was at the same time suggesting that not all behavior was volitional, or consciously organized and directed.

The issue of willfulness inevitably enters into our attempts to understand the behavior since the person *appears* to be func-tioning according to his own design and choice; the concept of instinct, however, implies that one has no choice except to alter it or modify it in some way.

The practical consequences of this postulate are extremely important. When one experiences anger in an interpersonal encounter there is a significant difference between assuming that the other person's intent was to make one angry, or recognizing that one's anger may have been the result of one's impatience and sensitivity. The first interpretation places the full responsiblity for one's reaction upon the other person. It does not take into account that anger may not have had to exist at all, that the reaction was related to factors inherent in oneself. The alternative way of examining such an event is to note the feelings and attitudes of both persons involved and to acknowledge that one's response is dependent on the other person's expectations and on one's own expectations and one's attitudes toward the other. It is necessary to explore the situation in detail to determine why the other person's intentions may have misfired. This approach recognizes the presence of out-of-awareness motives in one's behavior and does not overlook the possibility that one could, in fact, feel anger and express it in disguised ways. This approach also insists that the presence of motives must be established and does not merely assume them to be present because of theoretical preconceptions. Thus, a person may behave in an irritating manner because he has tender feelings toward the other person and fears that if he expresses them directly he will be hurt or humiliated. He may then become excessively coy, obsequious, or apologetic, which can be annoying. Although one might react with irritation to this person as well as to the one whose intent was to make one angry, tenderness is the underlying feeling in one case while anger is the prevailing effect in the other and when we play the game as do the psychoanalysts that tenderness is anger and anger is tenderness we may miss what really is going on. Similarly, the person who desperately wants to succeed, *because of his extreme anxiety to do so*, may bungle and perform ineptly. But he should be distinguished from the person who is unsuccessful because he has no real interest or desire to succeed. The indifference of the latter is manifest in his unsuccessful performance; the intent of the former is to succeed but his inordinate needs create so much tension and anxiety that he is unable to do so. The psychotherapist may be too ready to assume that, mentally ill or not, if a person tends to alienate others or to stir up unfriendly feelings toward himself, it is because he feels hostile and is therefore expressing it directly or indirectly. Although the view we are discussing may appear to deny the wish-fulfilling hypothesis of human motivation, it actually confirms it by taking into account the effect of anxiety in disintegrating efforts to fulfill one's needs. If a person's behavior is alienating because he feels hostile, it should not be called neurotic or pathological. His values may be skewed but he still proceeds to fulfill his goals directly, without compromise or conflict.

This way of looking at an event is a difficult one for the psychiatrist or social scientist with preconceptions about the motivations and the underlying drives of an individual. He utilizes a series of convoluted explanations to sustain the hypothesis and convince his patient that it is so. It is often easier for the patient to admit having hostile rather than tender feelings toward another person, especially a person of the same sex.

The ability to distinguish between intent and the consequences of behavior plagues the entire practice of psychotherapy. An endless search ensues to establish the underlying wish that promoted the behavior and produced the neurotic symptoms. Often the relentless and persistent efforts of the psychoanalyst may produce the very effects that he insists were already present in the patient's wishes. The patient may be pressed to examine and acknowledge aggressive elements in a piece of behavior in which he insists they are not present. The therapist's tenacious demand and his refusal to accept the patient's denial of such feelings may make the patient restive, annoyed, and ultimately, irritated and angry. Outbursts of anger, which may then follow, fail to prove that the anger was originally present in some transferential way or that the patient is truly aggressive. Instead, it may indicate that if pushed hard enough he can become annoyed and angry even though he began with feelings of some tenderness and warmth. This is a common enough drama acted out in the "who's angry?" game; one person is accused by another of being angry. Since he is not angry he responds with irritation and somewhat caustically says, "who's angry?". The other retorts, "You see? I was right. You are angry!" This is an example of the wish-fulfilling prophecy; we produce what we already expect and want to find in an interpersonal situation.

Neurotics often stir up anger and resentment in others when they really wish to promote good will toward themselves. When this is manifest in the extreme it is labelled "negative therapeutic reaction." It is often the therapist who goes into therapeutic negativism in his inability to handle this type of masochistic personality structure. The patient is behaving in the only way he knows, pressed by the dictates of his neurotic character structure. Certainly annoyance and despair are often stirred up in the therapist when he sees his potentially useful interpretations being distorted by the patient in destructive ways instead of the ways he, the therapist, intended. At times the therapist may feel so frustrated and helpless that he will terminate the therapeutic relationship and provide ample rationale and justification for the decision. In despair and disappointment the therapist describes the situation as the patient's unconscious need to fail.

The patient should not be blamed for behaving according to the dictates of his distorted thinking. The therapist's failure to distinguish patterns leads to a curious paradox. It is called "counter-transference" and we assume we understand it and never get caught in it. Unfortunately that is not so. But our very theory permits us to justify our counter-transference reactions and call them rational. The patient needs and wants therapy because of his repetitive tendency to fail and he is pushed out of treatment because this pattern of need to fail is also present in the therapeutic process. The term "negative therapeutic reaction" should be applied to a situation created by the therapeutic despair in the therapist not a defiant resistance in the patient. It represents a failure on the part of the therapist to be adequate to the task, whatever the reason may be.

How does this understanding affect therapeutic efficacy or the philosophy of change? The assumption that making the unconscious conscious, as illuminated by the wish-fulfilling hypothesis and the free association methodology could be the agent for behavioral and characterological change had to be abandoned by the evidence of failure in the therapeutic process. The need for a willful, determined commitment following the elucidation of the unconscious determinants came to be called the process of "working through." First it was thought that all that was necessary was to make the unconscious conscious; then, when it was found not to be enough, we added something called working through. In looking at the concept of working through, where does the concept of will and choice enter in?

How can the matter of will, choice or intention involve the therapeutic process when the philosophy of mental disorder is centered on the theory of unconscious drives and conflicts? Since the essence of a psychic defense is to avoid, deny, and make unavailable the real meaning and goal of behavior, how can we alter it by volitional means? If unconscious motivations do exist, then simple willfulness will not be enough to alter the behavior; one may not even be aware of which elements need to be altered. How can the patient control a dangerous impulse when he may not be able to identify its source or know what may trigger the response? Unless he knows the how and why as well as the nature of the impulse, he still cannot direct intentional capacities to prevent its appearance.

In spite of these apparent impediments to the volitional control of their impulses some patients have a strong drive and determined interest in overcoming them. Most people, however, prefer to remain as they are in spite of discomfort and limited productivity and display little interest in altering their way of life except at times of crises or great stress. Even then they wish only to eliminate the anxiety and not their way of reacting to it. They do not want to abandon their neuroses; they want bigger and better neuroses, but without anxiety. This is a striking feature in the obsessional disorders where anxiety and distress come from the unrealizable demand that the person be perfect and beyond human limitations. The recognition of weakness and fallibility produces the anxiety which may bring such a person to a psychiatrist.

Instead of trying to overcome his demands for superhuman performance, the obsessional patient wants the psychiatrist to perfect his neurotic structure so he will be immune to anxiety. If a more drastic change can be brought about in some magical fashion or moment or illumination without struggle, turmoil and only momentary discomfort, he might be agreeable to such a plan. Since the therapist is advocating change he often finds himself in the position of being viewed as an unacceptable and unwelcome authority figure. He appears to be encouraging change in areas in which the patient is only vaguely interested. When a person is motivated toward change there are many subtle, covert, and definable obstacles which may sabotage the process. Most striking is the evidence that though the patient may be strongly motivated to change he cannot alter his behavior or use his positive impulses for change in a constructive way because those aspects of his living require alterations which are beyond his conscious control and influence. Those compulsive elements in his behavior are precisely the ones he cannot alter by deliberate intent. This is the whole conception of therapy in discovering underlying issues that are involved in obsessive-compulsive behavior.

It has long been noted that insight alone is not enough to effect change in a patient's behavior. This observation led to a distinction between intellectual and emotional insight. Only the latter was assumed to have the power of altering neurotic behavior. Now we are aware that change requires an additional dimension.

What makes the difference is whether the insight is used and the degree of motivation that lies behind the efforts to use it. The therapeutic process must focus on the dual role of discovery and action, not merely on insight or understanding. Emotional insight may be viewed in this framework as decisive willfulness or committed intention. Change should be the ultimate goal in therapy. Unfortunately, it is not true that when a patient recognizes his neurotic pattern and uncovers its roots he will be free to experience in some magical way his new powers and will do so. The "working through," or the utilization of insight is a crucial aspect of therapy and frequently the most difficult one. This fact must be understood early in therapy, preferably through an actual experience in which a discovery about himself did bring about a favorable change in the patient's living. When the goal of therapy is change and not *just* insight, a more rational and organized treatment plan can be formulated.

This recognition raises the question of how much activity is justified in promoting and expanding the patient's volitional interests and wishes to effectuate a change in his living. Do such efforts have destructive possibilities in the ultimate resolution of the patient's neurosis? This, in turn, raises the equally controversial question of the value of resolutions, determined decisions and fervent promises and intentions in the achievement of one's goals.

The therapist's activity or passivity in the therapeutic process and the reliance on uncovering — in contrast to the exertion of will — as an instrument for change are questions that still need to be extensively investigated. Recent developments in ego psychology have directed attention to the issue of activity on the part of both patient and therapist and have already made meaningful advances in the permission to allow us to be more active. Frequently upon graduation from psychoanalytic institutes, those who carefully abided by the role of passivity as candidates change drastically for they find following the rules does not produce change in patients.

Some psychotherapeutic theories have insisted that while in treatment the patient should refrain from taking any steps or making any decisions or commitments about his or her life. They require that the patient talk out desires or intentions in the therapy sessions and refrain from "acting out." There are various justifications and rationalizations for this view, ranging from the need to allow the patient to arrive at his or her own goals after fully exploring all the neurotic obstacles and impediments in living to the notion that if acting out is prevented, the data that need to be discovered about these neurotic conflicts and anxieties will not be dissipated. This injunction implies that acting out or living and behaving according to one's neurotic patterns will interfere with the process of studying these patterns since the emotional elements in them will be expressed outside of the therapeutic sessions. Those who hold to this theory believe that the quality of the transference with the therapist is thereby reduced.

This viewpoint is justified if the theoretical assumptions which underlie it are valid. However, psychoanalysts do not universally agree that activity on the part of the patient or therapist disturbs or distorts the transference relationship. In some instances it may heighten it. Neither is it agreed that willful or decisive behavior in the course of treatment is always a neurotic device to avoid confrontation with one's unconscious. At times the patient's activity outside the therapeutic sessions may indeed be a way of frustrating treatment by avoiding a confrontation with his feelings and attitudes. This activity must be dealt with as a necessary part of understanding the patient instead of forbidding it to happen. The therapist's failure to interrupt impulsive and destructive behavior which may be an acting out of fleeting and transient feelings and attitudes can be most detrimental to the therapeutic process and ultimately, to the patient's existence. On the other hand, the patient must continue to function during the course of his prolonged therapy and some decisions can grow out of the encouragement and understanding achieved, long before a grasp of the total neurotic process is possible. It takes mature judgment on the part of the therapist to interrupt behavior when it is inappropriate and to allow it to proceed when it is useful. Rigid rules in this regard can be most detrimental, especially in the therapy of the obsessive-compulsive character disorders.

At some point in the process of therapy the patient must act on his new understanding and insight; activity must follow insight if progress is to occur. This understanding requires a reexamination of the role of will in a therapeutic process, obliging the therapist to restore its status as a force in human behavior which the concept of the unconscious has tended to minimize. It does not imply that the unconscious as a factor in human mentation should be abandoned or that one should resort exclusively to willful or conscious motivational factors in the therapy of the mental disorders. Some recent theorists have taken extreme positions in their zeal for behavioral alterations. Contrariwise, an awareness of the function of the will in human affairs will make it possible to avoid the excesses of those who advocate an exclusively unconscious origin to mental dysfunction and who see treatment as a process of mutual attunement and communication of the unconsciouses of empathic linkages of patient and therapist.

The problem is extremely complicated because in most neurotic states the will or capacity for committed intentionality is weakened. The patient feels helpless and hopeless, becomes very disorganized and demoralized. The patient is therefore handicapped in expressing his will at a time when his therapy requires him to exert it in order to make the necessary progress in undoing his neurotic, incapacitating patterns in living. On the other hand, many therapeutic approaches depend entirely on the patient's ability to mobilize his willfulness to effect behavioral changes without any alteration of his underlying character structure on the assumption that if things go on long enough the patient will raise the issue. These behavioral changes can be of the utmost importance in some circumstances but we must not confuse manipulation of a person's behavior with therapy of his neurotic or psychotic patterns of functioning.

The utilization of the patient's positive powers and his will to cooperate and participate can only enhance the therapeutic process when applied wisely. This is the dilemma of the psychotherapy process. By focusing on the areas of therapeutic interest one can negate the value of a free-floating, unfocused attention on the part of the patient and therapist. Awareness of this problem does not mean that it is necessary to establish rigid technical rules; rather, one must be free and flexible in one's attempt to artfully utilize both horns of the dilemma. The neurotic patient who is encouraged to "do" something about his distorted way of functioning is also warned against doing something called "acting out" or trying to alter his behavior by doing rather than talking. Sometimes this is good advice but also sometimes people try to solve all their problems by action. Some people try to solve all their difficulties by action and until they have learned enough about themselves, their activities will only repeat previous failures. On the other hand, refusal to take action in the face of new insight does not allow the patient to test out his discoveries to risk some unfortunate consequences. To get the support of the therapist in doing so is a necessary adjunct for any valid psychoanalytical work to be done. Unless the role of will in human functioning is taken into account, this contradictory situation will continue to plague psychotherapeutic theory and practice.

If, on the other hand, theories of personality development and psychopathology are determined by a multiple set of variables and a repeated set of experiences in a malevolent cultural environment one's expectations of a magical, immediate transformation of one's established patterns will be less likely. The therapeutic situation then becomes a partnership of two or more people (group or family therapy) and the process is one of attempting to understand how or why a person can be what he is, how his present way of living is maladaptive and unsatisfactory and how it can be altered without compromising or giving up valid goals and ideals. The individual is not required to adjust to a defective culture, but to adapt his skills and capacities to functioning more productively in it.

Because behavioral patterns tend toward stability and rigidity when successful in achieving their purpose the patient must be helped to develop positive motivations for change. To do this we must increase the person's self-esteem by a positive awareness of his true capabilities, divorced from neurotic idealizations and impossible expectations. Then he can see alternatives and choices heretofore blocked by compulsive needs. The expansion of his self through therapy enables him to choose. Such a process is long and arduous. It requires considerable skill on the part of the therapist to encourage his patient to utilize his resolve where the possibility of a successful outcome can reasonably be expected. We cannot wait for the *ideal* circumstances; they may never occur. Yet this is often the

115

patient's justification for postponing action. The therapist must take a calculated risk based on a reasonable understanding of the situation and the knowledge that if failure occurs, the patient will not suffer devastating effects, but may have a useful and necessary learning experience. This does not mean that we should encourage willful activity when the risks of failure seem too great or when failure might serve to confirm the patient's deprecated view of himself as an ineffective personality. To ask the homosexual to decide whether he wishes to live a heterosexual life before he has grasped any of the factors that produced his homosexuality will be useless and perhaps detrimental. Though he may wish to change in theory, pressure to get him to change before he is able to make a valid choice will only serve to strengthen his notions of inadequacy and incompetency.

One should always take into account the factors operating in a person's life that are beyond him, the realistic issue for example. The elements of compulsion which exist and operate in all mental illnesses as well as in so-called normal living must be taken into account in any attempts to alter inadequate patterns of functioning. If one's capacity for decisive action is interfered with by the compulsive need to behave otherwise no amount of persuasion or encouragement, however rewarding or punishing, will alter it.

How can we utilize our professional skills to formulate interpretations to patients whose disease patterns employ intellectualizing, philosophizing and conceptual thinking which is designed to defeat understanding? How can we focus on the concrete when the patient's defenses insist on generalization or when he concretizes to such a minute degree as to destroy the value of the observation? How can we ask a person whose disease prevents him from letting go or giving up control to abandon himself to the free association of "whatever comes to mind?" How can we manage to overcome a compulsion that is the essence of a rigid resolve by asking the patient to abandon all resolution and behave in a random, unplanned fashion, which he then turns into a new compulsion? These are the very questions that led me to get very interested in the compulsive states because the very pattern of traditional psychoanalytic methodology makes requirements of the compulsive patient, which is precisely antagonistic to the whole structure of his neurosis, which is designed to prevent that very thing. Consequently, the agreement that any psychoanalyst enters into with his compulsive patient, assuming that the compulsive patient can follow the rule, is just a farce because it is another device to behave in compulsive ways which defeats the very process.

These contradictions can be managed only when we recognize that the patient's behavior under these circumstances is *not* volitional and therefore cannot be terminated at will. In asking a compulsive patient to free associate we are asking him to do the very thing he cannot do. While we must not yield to his neurotic patterns or become enmeshed in them, neither can we become irritated, disappointed, or rejected because they continue. We must present the patient with a view of his behavior and its consequences without rancor or criticism and not assume that his behavior is the outcome of a conscious choice. He is a victim in the sense that there are influences outside his awareness that determine his behavior. The patient can experience some freedom in exploring different or more useful patterns of reacting only after these elements are clarified through the psychotherapeutic process and it is recognized that his rigid patterns are not necessary. Only then can we call on his commitment to change to attempt any alteration of those maladaptive, alienating ways of behavior that have produced his dissatisfactions, failures, and feelings of demoralization, helplessness and hopelessness. Then he can in fact be the master of his destiny, a total integrated self.

9

Configurational Analysis: A Method to Measure Change in Psychotherapy

Alan Z. Skolnikoff

In this paper I outline a method for studying change called configurational analysis. This method is described at length by Horowitz (1979). After explaining the development of the method and how it should be used in conjunction with therapy, I will suggest areas of research that would be crucial in determining change in therapy. Finally, I will give an extended clinical example to demonstrate the complexity of measuring change.

What are the reasons for developing configurational analysis? A method is needed to record and organize clinical observations that is not as abstract as the principles of metapsychology. The levels of abstraction or inference are confused in the usual case study. States clearly observed in a patient are often confused with what the therapist infers from his observations. Instead of directly describing what he sees, he infers what is being warded off. Interpersonal relationships or role relationships are not differentiated from internal self and object images. Information processing (unconscious defenses) is not differentiated from information control (conscious control mechanisms). In order to stay close to observations, configurational analysis focuses on terms such as states, role relationships, and information processing. Theoretically it has an object-relations and cognitive focus, but does not discount drives. State is defined as a person's current conscious self-image and inner model of relationship with another. The transition from one state to another is examined in terms of events, including internal control efforts to process or avoid information related to those events. Configurational analysis focuses on three periods of observation: (1) the patient before therapy, (2) the process during therapy, and (3) the outcome.

There are ten steps in analyzing a psychotherapy. These can be carried out in great detail (microanalysis) or applied to some specific features of the therapy or to the therapy more globally.

The first step involves establishing a problem list. Here the patient's initial complaints are separated from subsequent reports. Here we differentiate between those difficulties that can be observed but not recognized by the patient and those that the patient subjectively experiences. To give some perspective, the state of these initial problems can be compared with the state at the conclusion of therapy.

The second step involves listing the recurrent states that the person experiences, defining them by behavior observed and subjective experiences. Common shifts between states and their frequency and duration should be reported.

In the third step the self and object-role relationships are indicated in relationship to each state mentioned in the second step. This involves clarifying patterns of recurrent neurotic interpersonal relationships. One can infer the developmental level and its relationship to the current crisis.

In the fourth step the patient's experienced and warded-off ideas and emotions should be described. This should be gathered from observation (conscious reporting by the patient) and inference (unconscious control mechanism, with as little inference as possible).

In the next three steps the process is analyzed. In the fifth step the change in states is described with respect to how they occur in therapy, or in the patient's current relationships. When it is indicated, the therapist's emotional state should be described as well as that of the patient. (As with other parts of the study of the therapy, but particularly in this one, the states of the therapist-patient pair can be later studied by means of a videotape recording of a brief therapy.) Intervention by the therapist should be described in terms of how it influences the transition between states. How do external events, such as physical or chemical treatments that are ongoing, affect the changes in states of the patient?

In the sixth step development of the therapist-patient relationship should be described over time in terms of self-images and role models. Here the description of the therapeutic alliance, transference, and counter-transference should be described as it evolves throughout the therapy. Does the process continue after therapy is over? What is the effect of new relationships or separations on the patient?

In the seventh step an attempt is made to describe how the patient uses the information given in the therapist's interventions. Is it warded off, complied with, or denied? What effects do the therapist's interventions have on modifying the way the patient responds to his or her interventions? In other words, how do interpretations of the transference and/or the therapeutic alliance help the patient to modify controls?

In the final three steps the outcome is examined. In the eighth step the changes in the frequency and quality of the states are described. For instance, how do these changes interact with situational factors?

In the ninth step the outcome of changes in the self and object roles is analyzed. These changes should be related also to changes in interpersonal behavior patterns and support systems. One should describe what has not changed or has changed for the worse.

The tenth step involves a description of changes in coping and defensive styles. How are the central conflicting ideas and feelings now handled? This could be related to cultural attitudes and social values that are important in that person.

This method of configurational analysis has been extensively applied to two groups of patients: Those with posttraumatic stress disorders and patients experiencing bereavement. Usually we see people in psychotherapy because of a regression from a previously stable state. They have retreated from a relatively stable adaptive state to an unstable, maladaptive one. A successful outcome has been achieved if we can restore these patients to their premorbid state.

In contrast, in psychoanalysis we aim for a change in states. There is a systematic uncovering of conflicts that have led to arrested development. After these conflicts are understood and worked through in the transference and therapeutic alliance, development is permitted to continue in which entirely new states evolve.

The therapeutic alliance and transference can be examined through the development and change in role relationship models during therapy. This is particularly important in long-term psychoanalytic psychotherapy and psychoanalysis in which the deepening of the therapeutic alliance in conjunction with the exploration of the transference is considered essential to progress in treatment. The therapeutic alliance is defined as the optimal nontransference relationship achieved by the patient and therapist. Patterns that approach it and patterns that deflect from it can be studied. Transference and countertransference can be seen in relationship to and departure from the therapeutic alliance. There is considerable controversy as to how the therapeutic alliance can be fostered (Gill, 1982). This should be studied systematically. For example, various techniques that are advocated to promote the therapeutic alliance could be compared with others that focus purely on the transference. The evolution of the role relationships as observed in transcripts in a series of hours might be evaluated to determine what results are obtained by different techniques. Questions could be asked that would explain what a specific technique does or does not accomplish with different types of patients. This type of study of patient and therapist does not discard the intrapsychic model of a patient reacting to an optimally neutral analyst, whose interventions are primarily based on insight. Instead, we see in verbatim transcripts or in extensive process notes evidence of emotional interactions between patient and therapist. The therapist's and patient's capacity to understand this interaction leads to a strengthening of the therapeutic alliance. But to return to more specific questions of technique and how they alter the process and ultimately effect change in psychoanalysis, does the situation in which an analyst remains silent (denying gratification in order to promote regression) stimulate the establishment of the transference neurosis? The conflicting question is, must the analyst constantly interpret the patient's reaction to him within the psychoanalytic situation, even though his relative activity might be gratifying to the patient? Does this greater participation on the analyst's part postpone or hasten regression in the transference?

Another line of questioning challenges the centrality of the transference. Almost all classical Freudian psychoanalysts find the emergence of the transference, its interpretation, and its resolution the central features of a successful analysis. There appears to be nothing more convincing in the analytic process than to correct distortions of past memories by analyzing the current transference neurosis. But we have to ask the question, is the patient's capacity to use transference interpretations the only key to change? Or, is the transference just one very dramatic means of effecting change, others being extratransference interpretations, reassurance, or the observation of the emergence of various transferences with the avoidance of the interpretation of all negative ones. Does this relative avoidance of the transference fail to produce change as we define it in a psychoanalytic sense? Do idealizations of the analyst, which are not interpreted, detract from further development in the patient? Certainly, Kohut and his adherents avoid the premature interpretation of negative transferences. The emphasis on the evaluation of change in the Kohutian framework is the evolution of the narcissistic sector of the personality. Therapy is accomplished without interpreting the defensive nature of the idealizing and minor transference.

Studies could be done of verbatim transcripts to determine the relative efficacy of different techniques. Three categories of patients could be compared. In the first, the therapist would focus on transference interpretations wherever they were manifest in the psychoanalytic situation. In the second category, an analyst would pursue the transference in only those patients who appear to have the capacity to use the transference. In those who do not respond to transference interpretations or who respond negatively, a therapist would discreetly avoid the transference. In the third category, a therapist would avoid all transference interpretations, making interventions concerning present and past conflicts expressed by the patient without reference to the transference. One then might be able to judge which of these approaches would be most effective. Frances and Perry (1983) in their retrospective study point out that in brief focal therapy there are patients who can benefit from transference interpretations and those who cannot. Those patients who cannot benefit from transference interpretations do not necessarily have a poorer outcome. We can ask these questions prospectively, as indicated above, to determine if the resolution of the transference is a central factor in successful outcomes.

To return to the question of how to measure outcome and what constitutes positive change, an examination of outcome as outlined in the steps of the configurational analysis reveals that there are many different factors to assess. Symptom relief is often accompanied by an avoidance of areas of conflict. In those studies of outcome that focus on symptom relief and a reduction of anxiety and depression as an objective measure of a good outcome, some patients seem to have improved. Opposite results with the same patients can be obtained by focusing on a patient's capacity to face previously warded-off conflicts and tolerate increased anxiety and depression. Assessment of outcome with these criteria might give opposite results with the same group. A similar problem occurs when we attempt to discuss how situational factors in a patient's environment interact with changes that might have been effected by the therapy. We are often unable to decide how to weigh the influence of the therapy versus what appear to be chance occurrences in the patient's environment.

Other difficulties occur when we try to assess changes in a patient's self- and object images. As a result of prolonged treatment a patient may have made some modifications in self- and object images in connection with the resolution of previous conflict. For example, a male patient has conflicts concerning the relationship with his wife. If he stays with his wife, we have to assess as objectively as possible whether he has merely adjusted to his dislike of her (toleration of ambivalence) or has truly changed and modified his feeling of who he is and who she is in relationship to him. We face the same need to be objective in assessing a patient who leaves his wife as a result of treatment. We must differentiate between his avoiding a conflicted role relationship or his resolving to leave a regressed relationship to find a more mature one.

Similar difficulties occur when we attempt to describe the changes that occur in coping and defensive styles. Do we expect to see a change in core conflicts or, because of a greater understanding of the core conflict, do we see an increased ability to cope with conflicting ideas and emotions? An example illustrating this complexity would be a woman with a hysterical character who unconsciously seduces inappropriate men. A long treatment might help her to see and understand the reasons behind these seductions and perhaps help her gain some conscious control over the seductiveness. In a successful outcome we do not expect seductiveness to disappear; rather, we expect to see an increased capacity to cope with seductiveness with appropriate men, albeit with occasional anxiety.

I will now illustrate in an extended clinical vignette the treatment of a man whom I saw on two occasions in brief therapy and later in psychoanalysis. I hope to illustrate some of the complexities of assessing process and outcome in both psychotherapy and psychoanalysis. A single man in his mid-twenties, a computer salesperson, was referred by an internist who recognized that his presenting symptom was psychological. He was plagued for years by the feeling that other people thought he had a bad odor coming from his mouth. He thought this probably was not true because a variety of internists and clinics had studied this and found no physiologic evidence for the odor. He wanted to solve this problem though he doubted that talking about it would help. In an inquiry regarding when he first noticed the symptom, he reported that it started seven years before when he had an athletic scholarship to college and was on the baseball team. Following his first year, his arm felt weak and he decided not to turn out for practice. He felt ashamed and after this noted the first apperance of the bad odor. His mother had suffered from this kind of odor because of bad teeth. The father and his siblings had teased the mother about her condition. The patient experienced this symptom particularly when he had to convince a prospective client to buy the product he was selling or when he was trying to pick up a woman.

To pursue briefly some of the configurational analysis at this point: before the onset of the symptom, he felt like a confident masculine athlete. This state warded off another in which, if his athletic prowess was threatened, he could become a bad-smelling woman like his mother whom his father teased. This state of "smelly woman" might also relate to latent tendencies of wishing to be close to his father or other men, which would be warded off because of its homosexual implications. The symptom then was a compromise formation in which he warded off his passive feminine wishes by externalization. This permitted him to maintain his assertive masculine image despite occasional threats. The task in treatment would be to help him to tolerate some shift in states without an undue threat to his masculinity.

I interpreted that with his sore arm in baseball, or selling a product, or meeting a girl, he was ashamed if he thought he could not win. The symptom seemed to be a sense of embarrassment that he had about not getting respectful attention from the person he was trying to impress. The patient was intrigued with this interpretation and confirmed that his father often did not appear to be interested in his sports or the job he had even though he was enthusiastic in telling the father about them. He sometimes thought that the father felt this way about his body odor. In the next several weeks the symptoms diminished but did not disappear. Then I encouraged the patient to tell me in detail under what circumstances he had this symptom or whether it appeared while he was talking to me in the hour. At first he described work situations that confirmed the theory that he might have been embarrassed when he observed the feeling. One time, as he was describing his trying to meet a woman who was ignoring him, my attention wandered. He said, "I'm having the symptom right now with you. I think you think I smell." He was embarrassed to tell me this and I immediately recognized that he thought this about me because I was inattentive at that moment. I called this to his attention and he agreed that he noticed I did not seem to be interested just then. I was quite surprised that in the next few weeks this symptom completely disappeared. Accompanying this disappearance in the symptom, the patient had a mild depression and a diminution of ambition. He no longer was interested in pursuing women, which had been one of his favorite pastimes, and he did not think that he was that interested in pursuing a career in computer sales. I reassured the patient – and perhaps myself – by explaining that sometimes the disappearance of a symptom causes a mild depression, but I did not imagine that he would have any permanent difficulty around this. Indeed, in the ensuing three visits (I saw him at that time for a total of eight visits) that reassurance seemed to work and the patient returned to his normal activities with zest and without a reappearance of his symptom. He was appreciative for the removal of the symptom and agreed upon my request that he return in three months for a followup. I saw him for one session at three months, another at six months, and then at a year without any return of his symptom. We agreed not to have any further followup. At that time I was pleased that I had effected a symptom cure, although there seemed to be other features of his personality that we did not explore. This included his ambition, which did not seem clearly directed, and his pursuing women but never liking them that much once he had succeeded in conquering them.

When we apply this outcome to a configurational analysis, we can describe a shift in states, information processing, and self- and object images. With the removal of the symptom there is a diminution of driving ambition. He now tolerated more passivity with respect to his work and interest in women. He could now be a "relaxed guy," a state intermediate to an "assertive athlete" and "smelly woman." He now interpreted failures at work or in pursuit of women in a more casual way. Central to this change appeared to be a resolution of his feeling that I was not interested in what he was saying. He could now tolerate the idea that he need not interest me or colleagues at all times. He did not lose his self-respect as a man because of this. This brief therapy did not involve a change to new states but rather a greater degree of tolerance of warded-off states.

Two years later the patient returned with a new symptom. He thought that several male colleagues thought he was gay. I theorized that the latent homosexuality that was well-defended against by the previous symptom was now more directly expressed. Nevertheless, I proceeded to try to understand the context in which this symptom occurred and was similarly able to achieve symptom removal through analysis of the current conflicts and their links with the past, as well as some elements in the transference. As in the initial therapy, this one lasted eight hours. The outcome could be described in the same terms as the previous therapy. There appeared to be a greater tolerance of warded-off states of passivity previously associated with being feminine.

The patient then came back for a followup that we agreed to have three months later. At that time he stated, "I appreciate your having been able to deal with these symptoms I have, but there are deeper problems. I notice I'm never able to get closer to women, I really don't like my work, and I hate to present myself in a certain way in order to sell something that I'm not sure has any intrinsic value for me. I feel depressed a great deal of the time and would like to understand why this is. I miss my family, yet when I see them I don't feel as if they're really interested in me and I feel detached from them."

Here the patient presents himself without symptoms but rather with a general dissatisfaction with his work and the state of his relationships. He appeared more depressed than in previous encounters in therapy. Rather than adjustment to his current life situation he wanted basic changes to occur. In the decision to start psychoanalysis, we agreed that his previous adjustment was unstable enough to warrant a thorough exploration of his functioning, which might entail the production of new symptoms and an increase in anxiety and depression. I saw him for three years.

Very briefly, during the psychoanalytic treatment we uncovered warded-off states that explained his need to constantly maintain his assertive masculine image. He was made to feel like a "sissy" by his traveling salesman father whenever he lingered around the house with his seductive, smothering mother. His father also teased him about his interest in sports rather than productive work. Both maternal and paternal elements were present in the transference. On the couch he felt anxious about being lulled into passive seduction. He thought of many women with whom he had affairs who always wanted him to stay the night. He always felt soft and childish if he did. He felt this way when lingering with me. At other times he experienced me pushing him to work productively and teasing him about his lack of progress. He felt I thought he was stupid and lazy.

After extensive work on these warded-off self- and object images, a new, more stable state emerged. Instead of the "assertive athlete," he became a quieter, more thoughtful man. After treatment he changed his profession to a more passive one, led a more detached and contemplative existence, understood the defensive purposes of his compulsive heterosexuality, and no longer pursued women so actively. He developed his first long-term relationship with a woman in which he felt closer than he ever had before. He appeared more satisfied and less anxious in giving up grandiose ambitions in the sexual and work spheres. Now he had more of a sense of authenticity of his existence. Viewed from the outside, however, his family and friends thought he was worse off than when he started. Both his newly chosen profession, which gave him a lower income, and his wish to remain single for the time-being were viewed by his family and friends as maladaptive.

Comparing the outcome of the brief therapy with that of the long-term therapy raises many questions. One view is that as a result of a great deal of time and effort, I succeeded in fostering maladaptive solutions in a man who despite his anxieties and symptoms had been functioning reasonably well. During the three years of analysis, I often wondered why I had recommended this lengthy procedure with its indefinite results and longed for the purity of symptom relief and the brief encounters that I had had with him several years before. From another perspective, which involved both his and my personal assessment of the result, we noted a sense of genuineness. He now really liked his work. He was not ready to take on the responsibilities of marriage, but he was not plagued by his postponing this.

These changes as they are described are harder to define than those of brief therapy. In configurational analysis, we can attempt to describe them in a detailed way using objective criteria. By focusing on a state analysis in this patient, we see the beginning of a shift in states in the brief therapy sequences, with an unstable equilibrium, and finally a change in states accomplished during the analysis, with a more stable equilibrium. We can also describe the change in self-

and object images as well as information processing. The following is a sketch of some shifts in states:

Start of treatment. Predominant state — athletic, assertive male — dominating many women and aggressively competing with colleagues.

Warded-off state — smelly man-woman-sissy, passively unable to compete or interest women.

At end of brief treatment there is some modification of the warded-off state but this is unstable. Potential for depression is high.

Outcome of analysis. Predominant state — contemplative male — mutual relationship with one woman. Engaged in less competitive occupation.

Warded-off state — mild anxiety and depression about possible future marriage and career advancement.

This brief summary of some of the major states is a way of describing part of the change. To be more complete, changes in self- and object images as well as information processing should be described.

I hope I have illustrated some of the complexities involved in assessing outcome with this clinical vignette, as well as illustrating the different criteria for assessment applied to brief therapy and long-term therapy or psychoanalysis.

In this paper I have attempted briefly to describe the method of configurational analysis. Rather than focus on what constitutes change and what elements in the therapeutic process are centrally linked with change, I have tried to address questions about how we can better measure change and have consensual agreement that it has occurred. The central issue when we compare our observations of process and outcome has to do with developing a common language of observation. If we rely on metapsychology alone, we make complex inferences but do not achieve clarity of description. I have also suggested prospective studies that must be done to determine whether long-held beliefs concerning the importance of transference interpretations, and the relative activity or silence of the analyst are central factors in accomplishing positive changes in patients.

NOTES

Frances, A. and Perry, S. (1983) Transference interpretation in focal therapy. *Am J Psychiatry* 140:405-409.

Gill, M. (1982) *Analysis of the Transference*. Psychological Issue Monograph 53. New York: International Universities Press.

Horowitz, M. J. (1979) *States of Mind: Analysis of Change in Psychotherapy*. New York: Plenum Press.

10

Wider Differences: Dialogue IV

DR. ROBERT MICHELS (Moderator): We have had two responses to the previous psychological theories. Dr. Skolnikoff wants us to set aside our metapsychology and develop a new, less theoretically prejudicial, closer to clinical data, theoretical map rather than theoretical explanation, an organizing system for collecting our clinical experience so we can study it and use it to learn more. Dr. Salzman warns us that life is action and that there are elements in the theory of the mind that may, in therapy, lead to warnings against, or inhibitions of action. Making therapy another neurosis rather than a treatment for it, he persistently, doggedly, almost rigidly, reminds us not to be rigid as therapists. I ask the four people who were not presenting just now to comment.

DR. JEROME FRANK: Skolnikoff's clear, concise and clinically sophisticated exposition of configurational analysis opens up new possibilities for research in the field of psychopathology and psychotherapy. Conceptualization of the former in terms of states, their related self- and object-role relationships, and the experienced and warded-off ideas and emotions accompanying them, and analyzing therapy in terms of factors causing changes in states by means of configurational analysis promises to introduce a much higher level of objectivity into this field than customary psychodynamic formulations. It accomplishes this by reducing the necessity for inference to a minimum.

It is, of course, highly complex, and only research will determine whether it will be possible to catalog states and their accompanying features in such a way that they can be reliably identified — that is, that sufficiently high inter-rater reliability can be achieved. It remains unclear to me the extent to which configurational analysis implies any changes in the customary ways of doing therapy, as opposed to providing a different way of analyzing the therapeutic procedure.

The clinical example neatly demonstrates the difference between the relief of symptoms without change in life style and those accompanying a change in life style or, in Skolnikoff's term, a change in permanent states. It remains open to what extent the specific features of the analytic procedure are responsible for the change in permanent states and to what extent the role of the analytic framework is simply to provide a means of maintaining a prolonged, confiding relationship between therapist and patient. One could attribute the patient's change in life style essentially to prolonged acceptance by a person to whom he was attached of a less driven, more comfortable way of life accompanied by less need to maintain a hypermasculine self-image.

The case presentation does raise the important question of the implicit role of values of patient, therapist, and others in evaluating whether therapy has been successful.

Now it's hard to limit my comments on Dr. Salzman's paper because I agree with everything in it, so I think I'll just focus on one point. I think the most interesting thing he does is stress the importance of the will to change. Now, the argument between determinism and free will, of course, has gone on as long as people can think. And it's never going to be resolved. It's the beautiful example of that aphorism in philosophy: error never dies – but I think, for practical purposes, subjectively we all have free will, whether it is valid philosophically or not. What happens to our patients is their feeling of constraints on their free will. The more healthy you are the more you feel you are in control. That brings me then to the main point I want to make. I've got many of them here, but the word has just come into my vocabulary recently, perhaps one of the functions of the therapist is to empower the patient to exercise his free will. I think of an example I just had the other day which made more sense to me as I heard this discussion. It was a marital couple in therapy for quite a few years and they hadn't gotten very far because it turned out in retrospect the wife would yield in various ways to make things run better, but she always felt she was being coerced. And so, she would relapse and the husband, each time she would make these changes, would indicate that he didn't think it was going to last. He was really quite discouraged about it. Suddenly, something happened in two areas. One was the sexual one. She felt the normal wife would always be responsive to her husband sexually and at times she didn't feel responsive but she couldn't tell him this. They would start lovemaking and she would raise all kinds of objections and things which got him more and more irritated and upset. Well, I sent her to a sex therapist just once. She disliked him intensely. The relationship didn't work, but he assured her, you see from his authority, that her behavior was perfectly normal. That is, it wasn't abnormal not to be aroused all the time and suddenly the whole problem disappeared. She became responsive all the time because she no longer felt coerced. And the other example that is even more striking to me: one of her patterns that irritated her husband to death was that she spent an awful lot of time reading trash novels, to the point that she didn't get her housework done. Several times she would stop, and then she would relapse, so he would become quite discouraged. But, suddenly one day something happened. She decided she could stop, and she stopped. It's like giving up smoking. Within a couple of weeks she didn't want to read anymore. Now I don't know what I did to bring that about, but it clearly happened. In other words, when the patient feels that she is in charge, then things work well. It all illustrates that old joke about lightbulbs. One of the lightbulb stories is, How many psychotherapists does it take to change a lightbulb? And the answer is, Only one, but the bulb has to want to change.

DR. JERRY LEWIS: Dr. Skolnikoff's paper does represent an exciting attempt to operationalize constructs central to psychoanalysis and psychoanalytic psychotherapy. If successful, it would greatly increase our understanding of factors involved in the process of successful treatment.

The critical issue that the paper does not address sufficiently is suggested in the author's statement regarding consensual agreement. Given that the constructs suggested are less abstract than many metapsychological premises, can observers independently agree as to their presence and intensity? If, for example, we have verbatim transcripts or videotapes of Skolnikoff's work with the young man whose treatment is summarized in the paper, would we agree about the presence of predominant and warded-off states and their changes? It is this movement from the therapist's observations to those of independent observers or raters that is crucial for the next stage of development of configurational analysis.

As we move toward the end of this conference, I'm again, as I am so often in so many of my activities, impressed with the difficulty that we have in maintaining a shared focus that says there are many roads to Rome. The tendency among all of us to move into dialectics that are either/or concerns me. I felt some of that during this conference. As we hear intriguing and exciting ideas and concepts that differ from our own, although we all acknowledge that multiple variables are involved, that various combinations of variables may be involved with different patients, and that cure, whatever that means, can be arrived at in many different ways, I think there is a tendency for us to think in terms of either/or, or kind of oppositional tendencies and, in some ways, I think the process of our interaction is terribly important. I appreciated both of these papers greatly because they gave me cause to think. They made me question some of my ideas or gave me some new ideas about things I can do when I get home. I found myself having a fantasy, however, during this session. I wonder how much polarization would have occurred if we were less alike and more different in our conceptual orientations, if, on this program, we had had a behaviorist, a cognitive therapist, or if we had had some people who share less commonalities with us in terms of the evolution of our own thinking.

DR. PAUL ORNSTEIN: I was told at one time, when I was in Italy, that there were many roads to Rome. I tried to take several of them and I never got there. Finally, somebody suggested that route 275 would get me there and I arrived in Rome. I listened very carefully and attentively to Dr. Salzman's exposition. I found in it several – actually, to be exact, seven – beautiful little clinical nuggets of wisdom embedded in a sea of confusion: because Dr. Salzman claimed that he was going to give us a clinical paper. Yes, he did give us clinical nuggets, but he misled us, in a way, on an epistemological level by saying that he was more atheoretical than either Paul Dewald or myself. I think he is just as theoretical but he uses implicit theories that he does not make explicit and, therefore, is somewhat confusing, because we don't know what is the total structure from within which he talks. Therefore, I believe, until he has the courage to give us a more explicit and systematic theory in which he can give us his clinical wisdom and knowledge and effectiveness, we will not be able to learn from it. We will become confused, but don't despair – I certainly don't. I generally do not ward off confusion. I try to live with it, taste it, reflect on it and hope for some resolution. So I do feel positively about Dr. Salzman's paper for two reasons. I always wanted to encounter him personally and I did. And now I'm going to take home the paper and will live with the confusion while I try then to straighten out some clinical theory he has in it.

DR. PAUL DEWALD: In some ways Dr. Skolnikoff's paper might have been the initial one in this program since he provides us with a framework in which to discuss some of the issues raised in this panel. I think very cogently he points out how complex and multi-factorial is the process of evaluation. I agree with him completely that one must look not only at the manifest behavior but also at

137

some of the meanings which this behavior has for the patient, both consciously and unconsciously, and that it is essential to hook our assessments and evaluations to clinically demonstrable and observable phenomena. It is also, I think, essential to separate data from the therapist's inferences, in as much as the same behavioral data may be subject to multiple different inferences.

He goes even beyond this, however, in terms of providing us with at least one version of a methodology for doing the kinds of evaluations he had described. I am impressed by the dynamic way in which his methodology can be applied and also by the absence of stereotypes and clichés couched in theoretical models or language. If we are to progress in our efforts to understand what we are doing, we must have a methodology which is repeatable, which is more than impressionistic, which can pinpoint specific elements of the process, which recognizes the enormous complexity, and which is reproducible so that others using the same data can arrive at differing conclusions.

My main disagreements with him focus around the distinction he makes between psychotherapy and psychoanalysis. He is describing a specific form of psychotherapy with posttraumatic stress disorders and patients who were experiencing bereavement, but I think that the process is applicable in a significantly wider group of patients, and, therefore, a number of significant and apparently permanent changes in what he calls "states" can occur. In other words, I believe that in many instances, psychotherapy does more than "restore these patients to premorbid state." The other area that I would have some doubts and questions about is his recommendations for experimental study in some of these issues. I am doubtful that one could separate patients in such a way as to utilize specific, experimentally determined forms of technical intervention (for instance, focusing exclusively on transference, or, in another instance, avoiding the transference) and still maintain anything like a naturalistic process. We have to be careful that in studying the process we do not alter it too much. However, I do agree with him that we do need to have recordings of the primary data if we are eventually going to delineate the specifics both of the treatment process itself and the evaluation of it after it is concluded.

All in all, I think that Dr. Skolnikoff has pointed out an important path for us to follow in the future, and the kind of research that he is advocating will be increasingly crucial if we are to demonstrate the efficacy of psychotherapy to those who make important policy decisions in our society.

And in regard to Dr. Salzman's paper I had many, many disagreements with it and I don't see that there is any point in itemizing them. I think, however, the way I would describe what he says is that he has used examples of poor therapy, of poor therapeutic technique, of issues that he calls analytic, that I would not call analytic. The therapist who badgers, who insists, who demands that he knows better than his patient, the other various manifestations and all its caricatures that he offers as if these were valid examples of what we would think of as optimal or reasonable psychoanalytic techniques. . . . I would point out using a metaphor that doesn't tell us anything, that doesn't prove anything, that there are surgeons who, from time to time, do cut the common bile duct when they are taking out the gallbladder or do sever an artery that they should not have severed. That does not discount surgery as a procedure. The fact is they are poor surgeons. There are poor psychoanalysts, there are poor therapists, but that does not in any way eliminate or prove or disprove the validity of some of the underlying basic principles. That's about as much as I think I can say.

DR. ROBERT MICHELS: I'm going on the basis of simple humanity, to allow single sentences if they want them from our two presenters.

DR. ALAN SKOLNIKOFF: A brief response to questions raised by Dr. Lewis and Dr. Dewald. We can get consensual agreement between independent judges when we confine ourselves to clinical observations. When we attempt to make inferences about warded-off states or layering of defenses, there is much less consensus. So far, configurational analysis has been applied to brief therapies with clearly defined treatment goals. Longer treatments with less defined goals pose a greater problem for consensual validation. By focusing on specific themes and studying videotapes at intervals in treatment, we hope to obtain considerable agreement between judges.

I agree with Dr. Dewald that we cannot set up experimental design that would lead to artificial therapies. However, we can take therapists of opposing persuasions and have them treat similar categories of patients comparing process and outcome in both groups.

I would like to make another remark though, about Dr. Salzman's paper. It seems to me that one of the things that we haven't focused on, except that Paul Ornstein did for a moment at the beginning of his presentation, is the setting in which we developed our theories. We have to remember that Dr. Salzman developed many of his ideas, at least I would suspect he did, by working with very difficult obsessive-compulsive patients. It is entirely possible that some of the ideas that he is describing would apply specifically, and develop from his work with those patients in which certain maneuvers in the middle of a long therapy, which would involve more action than the will that he's describing, would be very useful. Whether or not those can be applied to all neurotic patients in all situations is another question. But, let's not forget that that might be where these ideas originated and in that sense, many more of us would agree that in these situations, these ideas are more useful.

DR. ROBERT MICHELS: Dr. Salzman, one long sentence.

DR. LEON SALZMAN: Yes, I think that's true, my ideas mostly have been developed out of the obsessive-compulsive, but Freud's developed out of the hysterical. So each of us has a bias. The point that Dr. Dewald makes, I want to clarify. I was not talking about the psychoanalyst who pursues the kind of program that Dr. Dewald has described, but, unfortunately, I must say that there are not too many of those around. I'm talking about the psychoanalysts who are colleagues of mine, who are graduates of institutes, who are pursuing therapeutic programs that do, I'm sorry to say, resemble perhaps the slightly hyperbolic in my description. I really do not mean to imply that there are not competent Dewalds and Ornsteins and other psychoanalysts who do not.

Summation

11

Robert Michels

My problem in trying to summarize these interactions is that so much was said that I will have to leave a great deal out of the summary. In some ways it is much like the task in psychotherapy — there are so many things going on that the problem isn't in finding the theme, it's selecting a theme. It isn't figuring out what the interpretation might be, but it's discarding many of the interpretations that obviously could be used and selecting the one that seems best. That is how I think of psychotherapy and also the way I react to the presentations we have had today.

First of all let me talk about change. I'm going to shift from cure to change; it feels more comfortable and I think most of the presenters tended to talk more about change than cure. Although the words can be interchanged, they are not synonymous. Change occurs in life in all kinds of situations and the models that most theorists of psychotherapy have used in talking about change come from a variety of areas of change in life outside of therapy. One way of understanding what the different panelists have said is to try to detect the model of change outside therapy that they are using implicitly as the prototype for change in therapy. For some of the panelists this is easy; for others not quite so easy. For example, one kind of change that occurs in life is the change of development; people change between birth and maturity. There is immense change between infancy and the years of ten or twelve for a boy or girl. This offers a powerful model of change and it is a model that informs some concepts of psychotherapy. We see it most clearly in Dr. Ornstein's model of how treatment works. Treatment for him is a second chance at a developmental process that was arrested or went awry the first time around. This model of treatment as an opportunity for the resumption of arrested development also has in it implications for what therapists do. Therapists are surrogate mothers. They provide the substrate, the nutriment (for Ornstein the empathic nutriment) that is essential for development to go well. If a developmental course that didn't go well the first time is to be corrected and get back on the track, the empathic nutriment must be provided the second time. The job of therapy is to create the second opportunity for personality development when something went wrong the first time. It's a clear model of change.

Change also occurs within intense meaningful relationships. Psychotherapy involves an intense meaningful relationship, and models of change in relationships can be used for explicating change in therapy. In his paper Dr. Lewis doesn't address this model directly, but he is certainly talking about the importance of intense intimate relationships as stabilizing factors in psychic functioning. The modification of such a relationship – in his paper a marital relationship – becomes a way of changing psychic functioning. In a sense, Dr. Lewis' paper is about a corrective emotional experience displaced outside of the transference onto a contemporary relationship in the patient's real life. The therapist manipulates that relationship in order to facilitate change. It's the kind of thing one might do as the therapist of a young child, arranging for a foster family or an adoption or advising a teacher or tutor.

A third model of change in life is change that occurs at times of crisis. People change under intense stress. Such stress might be an overwhelming threat to life, a physical illness or some other global stress. Dr. Horowitz has written about responses to such stress and we hear from Dr. Skolnikoff, a member of Dr. Horowitz's group, about stress response changes as one model of change. The model is complicated and requires familiarity with some new terms.

The dominant model for this group is clearly psychoanalysis. When you assemble a group of psychotherapists and ask them to talk about change in psychotherapy, they slide into talking about psychoanalysis so quickly that it is hard to remember that there are other theories of psychotherapy, other strategies of approach. Even the least psychoanalytic of our presenters, Dr. Frank, assures us that he too has been analyzed, that he too has been touched by the experience, and that he too knows something about what it is about.

The purest presentation of the classical psychoanalytic position that we have heard is from Dr. Dewald and I suspect that he feels no discomfort with either the words pure or classical in that sentence. He emphasizes that in the classical formulation of the psychoanalytic theory of change each of the factors that I have mentioned can be seen as one component of a complex multi-determined system. There are developmental aspects to the change process in psychoanalysis, but unlike Ornstein, Dewald does not elevate development to the architectonic principle of change in psychoanalysis. He sees it as one aspect of change. There are relational aspects. Dewald emphasizes, to my ear more strongly than most classical analytic thinking, the importance of the interpersonal relationship between the analyst and the patient as an agent of change, but here again he does not elevate it to a single dominant position. There are also aspects of stress and response to crisis. In a way the transference neurosis is an iatrogenic disease fostered by the treatment in order to exploit the potentials for change that are found in disease and crisis. If the patient can't suffer he can't get better as the result of treatment and Dewald points that out clearly. In keeping with classical analytic thinking he exploits all three of the models of change I've mentioned while balancing them and remaining free to shift from one to another as the specific case or situation or episode demands.

Drs. Frank and Salzman remind us that most of life takes place outside of treatment, that we don't know how treatment works, and they urge on us the oldest of medical warnings *primum non nocere*, above all do no harm. Dr. Salzman particularly tells us that patients need to act in the world. They have the capacity within themselves for healing and for growth and we must be exquisitely careful in our therapy not to interfere with the potential for cure that is within our patients, not to stifle or constrain or restrict their possibility for change whatever its source might be. I think that he stands in awe and silence about what that source is. He warns us to facilitate and support the patient's own mechanisms of change with the implicit or at times explicit suggestion that too strong a belief on our part about how therapy works, particularly in the absence of any real knowledge about how therapy works, may be dangerous. I hear him suggesting, and I think Dr. Frank agreeing, that when one doesn't know, it is wise to be openly ignorant rather than to pretend knowledge that may stifle and that may be wrong.

Let me shift from speaking about change to speaking about treatment. For our group there is pretty good agreement on what treatment is, not how it works, nor even whether it works, but what it is. If they had an opportunity to look in on a patient and a therapist, I don't think they would argue among themselves about whether or not psychotherapy was going on. They might argue whether it was good therapy but they would agree whether or not it was therapy. Therapy involves a relationship and it involves a goal of helping or changing somebody. It involves an asymmetric relationship with the therapist being an expert at something, having some special knowledge or skill or ability or awareness that has to do with human relationships. It involves mentalism. There is no shame about that in this group. When you try to help somebody with psychotherapy you're trying to get inside that person's mind and change his psychic life. There is no behaviorist on this panel. Therapy involves talking and communication, symbols and meanings. They would agree that psychotherapy is all of these things.

We should make explicit that the panel is not about certain things. It is not about the question of the efficacy of psychotherapy. This group assumes that at least there are some conditions or circumstances in which psychotherapy is probably effective. Indeed the evidence at present is that it is pretty generally effective in many different circumstances. There is much more controversy about whether it has any specific as opposed to nonspecific effect, whether it is simply the world's most elaborate placebo or whether it is more than a placebo. Dr. Frank addresses this directly, questioning specificity while the other panelists by implication take a strong position supporting it. One would not worry as much about the details of the various different theories we have heard if one believed that the theories didn't make any difference. The specificity/nonspecificity issue is not yet resolved. There is no convincing scientific data that argue for specificity, but I would remind you of Dr. Frank's warning that the methodologic problems of demonstrating specificity are such that even if it were there we probably would not have found it in the data currently available to us. Where might we look? There are two obvious possibilities. We can look at the patient or we can look at the therapist. If we look at the patient, we can look at his disorder or at other factors about his personality, his cognitive style, his psychological make-up, social culture factors or nondisease factors. If we look at the therapist, again we can look at him as a person or we can look at his theory, technique, strategy or method. Most of our time here has been spent talking about the therapist's theory and method. We have not talked as much about the other places we might look. We haven't talked about the nontheoretical aspects of the therapist, such as his personality or cognitive style. There was one interchange with Dr. Frank about that, but we didn't return to it. We also might look at the patient's disorder. We haven't been talking about the treatment for depression or any other specific disorder. Dr. Dewald told us that his treatment, in its narrowest definition, is suitable for 5 to 10 percent of people. Dr. Ornstein told us his treatment is suitable for much more than 5 to 10 percent of people although it is really a spectrum of treatments. Dr. Lewis, in the case he presented to us, certainly indicated that at least on a health/sickness scale he is willing to treat a fairly wide range of patients. However, we haven't talked about specific mechanisms of change related to specific disorders. Finally, and again only Dr. Frank alluded to this, there are nondisorder aspects of the patient as well as the therapist that may be significant. Dr. Frank is one of those wonderful people who turns things upside down and makes them more interesting. Everyone else in the field worries about selecting the best treatment for a specific disorder. Frank says we are all wrong; the disorder doesn't make any difference or perhaps there really is only one disorder and further, the theory doesn't make any difference because nobody understands it except the therapist and usually he is confused as well. What really makes the difference are other factors in the patient, his cognitive and personal style, and other factors in the therapist, his enthusiasm, commitment, availability, and devotion, and particularly the fit between the two. When you do research on diseases or theories, you're doing research on twiddle-dedums and twiddle-dedees, rather than studying the real determinant of the outcome of treatment, the human relationship between patient and therapist.

How does therapy work? Everyone agrees that therapy works in many ways; there isn't a single mechanism of action. That in itself is very important. Even when we hear a paper on a specific mechanism, such as Dr. Lewis' presentation, we note his opening paragraph which states that there are many mechanisms. Each person recognizes that his special view does not encompass the totality of all that is going on in psychotherapy. Everyone also agrees that there are important nonspecific aspects to how treatment works. To put it in an exaggerated and polarized way, one view is that the nonspecific aspects lead to the therapeutic effects. I believe this is Dr. Frank's position. For him the theory of psychotherapy is sort of like the basket that's made in an occupational therapy session. It's not the basket that helps the patient, it's the sense of pursuing a task with the collaboration of another person who is helping and teaching and participating together with the patient, working and sweating, making errors and correcting them, and finally achieving something. The process is therapeutic, not the basket; it doesn't even have to be a basket. For Dr. Frank, psychoanalysis or behavior therapy or gestalt therapy are three different kinds of baskets. It may be important that the therapist loves the basket but we don't have to be fooled by that as we watch therapy from outside. On the other end of the extreme we find Dr. Dewald and Dr. Ornstein who on this issue join very comfortably together. The purpose of the nonspecific aspects of the therapeutic situation for them is to set up the context in which the specific aspects can work. The nonspecific aspects create the relationship in which the transference can emerge. They create the alliance in which it can be interpreted. They create the context in which the possible negative effects of the regression can be controlled and bounded so that they don't lead to disaster. The nonspecific aspects of treatment are, in Dr. Dewald's terms, facilitating of the specific effects. It is a very different model from Dr. Frank's although the concepts they use are quite similar: relationship, understanding, and so on.

When we talk about the specific mechanisms that might work I think it is important to note that there may be different mechanisms for different therapists, for different patients, or for different theoretical strategies of how to do therapy. For example, there is one point of view that psychoanalysis works on fantasies, but that psychoanalysis as a psychotherapy may not offer much help for the direct impact of trauma on the individual unless that impact was mediated by fantasy. I believe that is the traditional belief. Today Paul Dewald might accept that version but I doubt that anyone else on this panel would be happy with it.

Another example is that severely rigid patients may require not only symbolic interventions and activities on the part of the therapist but also nonsymbolic activities as well. The full elaboration of this view would be the notion that for severely rigid patients who transform words into nonmeaningful experiences that are monotonous, repetitive, and unmutative, words alone will never help. This is Dr. Salzman's position as stated in my language and, as pointed out by Dr. Skolnikoff, it is a position that stems from an idea of one of Salzman's teachers, Harry Stack Sullivan, who described patients who use language to avoid communication. These are the severe obsessionals. One can't really communicate with them in words because they are masters at making words obstacles to communication. So Salzman does something else. Does he kick them or stroke them, or perhaps both at times? We are not sure from what he said, but it's clear that he doesn't believe that talking is going to be enough.

A third example is that some therapists may have special empathy for special patients, and when one of those lucky matches occurs miraculous things happen. As Jerry Frank told us, the statistics fail to show specificity. But anyone who has been in the business for a long time has seen one or two cases where there was no question that after years of suffering and disaster there was a click, a therapist that matched the patient, and what seemed to be a miracle. Some therapists have accomplished a few of those miracles and those of us who have known them well sometimes suspect that it's because they are treating their own disease at the same time they are treating the patient's and that they have a special empathic understanding as a result. I sometimes suspect that you can't treat someone if you haven't in some way shared in that disease yourself. When we look for mechanisms of how therapy works, we don't have to look for extreme reductionist mechanisms. We don't have to look for the single mechanism that explains how psychotherapy works for everyone, for it doesn't exist. We should look for a family of mechanisms, one or the other or some combination of which may be involved in some of those situations where there is a specific effect of psychotherapy in addition to the generally available non-specific effects of psychotherapy.

Let me mention the presentations and comment briefly about each of them. Dr. Lewis emphasizes one type of change, in which the patient's world is manipulated by the therapist who influences some significant other in the patient's life. Since we live in social worlds and our intrapsychic structure is maintained interactionally in a series of transactions with real people around us, significant others maintain our psychic structure. If the therapist can arrange a change in an important person in the patient's life, either through the patient or directly, then that change may reverberate back into a change in the patient's psychic functioning. This is a standard model of one type of treatment, the treatment of children. Who would imagine treating or even psychoanalyzing a child without some contact with the family and usually some attempt to deal not only with the intrapsychic determinants but also with the real relationships in the child's life that are maintaining his pathologic functioning. Dr. Lewis is treating his patient as if she were a child, and if she were seven years old there would be nothing remarkable about the type of intervention that he used. I've already raised one problem with this model (Dialogue III), revolving around the assumption that insofar as psychotherapy is the treatment indicated the rate limiting factors in change or cure are not the behavior of others but intrapsychic factors in the patient that either overwhelm the reality of others and replace them with imagined objects or that control the real others and force them to play assigned roles in the patient's neurotic transference fantasies. If this woman could best be helped by having her husband change his behavior then the indicated treatment was not psychotherapy at all and one might ask why even bother seeing the woman in the first place since her problem was no more intrapsychic than if she had a thorn in her shoe. There is good treatment for a thorn in one's shoe and it is highly effective, but it is not psychotherapy. However, if you have a thorn in your shoe and because of some neurotic problem you don't remove it, then there are two ways to proceed. One is to have the therapist take it out, which cures the foot but not the neurosis. The other is to be analyzed so that you learn why you're afraid to take it out yourself and eventually you pull it out. This cures the foot, somewhat more slowly it is true, but it also changes your life from that point on. These are two different and competing models of therapy.

Dr. Frank speculates primarily about the nontechnical characteristics of the therapist, about the fit or complementarity between the patient's personality and cognitive style and those of the therapist. Dr. Frank really believes that we treat a single disease and he doesn't think very much either of the technical aspects of our theories and the interventions they prescribe or of the importance of the subcategories of that particular disease.

Drs. Dewald and Ornstein speak about the psychoanalytic approaches to treatment. I've never used that phrase before, but isn't it nice to think that there are now psychoanalytic approaches to treatment and that the plural is acceptable in our maturing field. Each of them emphasizes that psychoanalysis is a model for all dynamic psychotherapy. Dewald emphasizes the nonspecific factors that facilitate the therapeutic situation. He believes that the situation involves regression in the paradoxical setting of a nonneurosogenic therapist while the individual's original infantile state was in the presence of a neurosogenic parent. Because of this paradox between the similarity of the regressed state and the infantile state and the difference between the therapist and the neurosogenic parent, the patient gains insight, with the help of the therapist's interpretative assistance. The result is the resolution of psychic conflict which is central to Dewald's model. Developmental arrest may be present and treatment may facilitate the resumption of development, but if developmental arrest is present it is understood as secondary to psychic conflict. Ornstein in contrast sees arrested development as primary. For Ornstein, if psychic conflict is present, he believes it is most probably the result of a disturbance of development rather than the other way around. For Ornstein arrested development leads to conflict. For Dewald conflict leads to disturbances of development. Empathy, a nonspecific factor for almost everyone else on the panel, becomes a specific factor for Ornstein because empathy is the critical ingredient that allows the resumption of arrested development. The task is to get the infant, whose development was arrested, to grow again. Insight and the internalization of certain aspects of the relationship with the therapist are relatively secondary for Ornstein, epiphenomenal to the central mechanism of how therapy works.

Skolnikoff introduces a kind of metasystem or regulatory system to our thinking. His patient has a series of states, a deck of cards. Skolnikoff's treatment doesn't do much with the states themselves, but it does a great deal with the shuffle. He influences how and when and for how long each state emerges and the transformation functions that determine when a state is initiated or terminated. He doesn't discuss it, but it is interesting to speculate about whether one might distinguish psychotherapy from psychoanalysis because psychotherapy leaves the individual cards alone and tries to alter the shuffle while psychoanalysis tries to get into the states themselves and perhaps have some influence in modifying them.

Dr. Salzman uses terms that embarrass most psychoanalysts. Not since Otto Rank have we heard "will" spoken of at a conference on psychotherapy as many times as it appears in his paper. He points out the age-old paradox of dynamic psychotherapy. Our goal is to help the patient to gain free will and autonomy and the enhanced capacity to shape his own life. However, our theory says there are no such things as free will or autonomy and the belief that one has them is really a delusion common among people who want to deny the powerful determination of psychic drives. How do we live with this paradox? Most of us have learned to live with that problem or we couldn't remain in business. The paradox goes back well before psychoanalysis; it was clearly formulated by Immanuel Kant and has not been resolved in philosophical disputes since that time. Salzman studies a patient population for whom that paradox is paralyzing and his management of it becomes central to his treatment. There is danger in generalizing from special populations. Although the paradox exists in every psychotherapy, it is the central field of therapeutic effort or inquiry in only a small number of treatments.

Psychotherapy is smaller than life. We get into trouble when we forget that. There are more problems that cannot be dealt with by psychotherapy than there are problems that can be. When psychotherapy is effective, it changes one or two or three percent of the things that shape one's destiny. That is not very much unless it is you, and if it is you it's a great deal. But either way it is only a small amount compared to what cannot be touched by psychotherapy. Freud had no doubt on that issue. If you have the choice of controlling your destiny or selecting a good therapist, control your destiny! Psychotherapy deals with the mind, with what Frank calls the realm of meanings and the assumptive world, with what I call, meaning much the same thing, psychic reality. If some feature of the patient's mental life is not an important factor in the problem, then psychotherapy is not the right prescription. That is a simple rule. If there isn't a problem in your mind, you don't need psychotherapy. If a patient says my real problem is in the outer world, either you think the patient is wrong, as you commonly do, believing that the statement is defensive or projective, or else you don't advise him to get psychotherapy. Problems in the mind are often important complications to all kinds of other problems in life. What Frank calls demoralization is an example of this. In those cases in which problems in the mind are secondary to nonmind primary problems, I believe therapy is often useful largely as a result of nonspecific factors, the support and the antidemoralization aspects of therapy. However, at times problems of the mind are not secondary to other problems; they are primary. If problems in the realm of the psyche are primary and if psychotherapy works, as it occasionally does in these situations, I believe that it is the specific rather than the nonspecific factors that make the difference. I don't know of any single simple formula for how these specific factors work, but we can say a few things about them. First, they have to have impact after and outside of the sessions. If the treatment only influences the patient's behavior in the therapist's office, there is no important therapeutic effect. Second, they have to persist after the treatment. I would agree with Freud's position in "Analysis Terminable and Interminable" (Freud 1937) that it is too tough a test to say that they have to be permanent, irreversible, and that the pathology should never reappear. Where else in medicine or in life do we require that before applauding a treatment? Third, they do not have to involve understanding. Insight is a mechanism, not a goal of psychotherapy. Insight itself never cured anything except ignorance. However, although insight and understanding are not essential, therapy does involve change in the patient's mind, in his world of meanings, in his psychic reality. By whatever language we use, cognitive maps, coping strategies, mental structures, the result must involve stable and persisting changes in the patient's mind. They may be similar to developmental changes, to changes that occur in learning, to changes that occur in conversion experiences, to posttraumatic changes, or to relational changes. I suspect that in most therapies most or all of these factors are combined if the therapy is to be truly successful. Psychoanalysis in general spends much more time creating the context for these factors to work, the relationship, the alliance, the transference neurosis, than it spends on the specific interpretative interventions that are designed to foster change.

Many of our theories of psychotherapy are helpful for a small number of patients; none of them works for most patients. We have to search for more powerful theories that work for larger groups, but we also have to recognize the need to keep a sufficient number of theories around so that we can deal with the variety of people who seek our help. If you want to protect a pure theory you must narrow your practice to a very small range of patients. I suspect that some of our purest theorists have managed to stay pure by exactly that maneuver. If a therapist wants to be theoretically pure, he must have a referral source who screens out most patients and sends him only people who fit his theory. That's not necessarily bad; those patients often do well, but we ought not be misled into thinking that because a theory works with highly selected patients, it tells us something fundamental about human nature.

As a metaphor for how psychotherapy might sometimes work, consider a well known episode from a different area of life. When Helen Keller first learned language, she was no longer an infant. She wasn't a young child learning language, or an older child learning a second language, but rather an older child learning a first language. It changed her life and her world. It had immense impact on her relationships with others, on their responses to her, on who she was, and on what she was to become. Nonspecific factors were essential for this to be possible — trust, warmth, love, a human relationship. Those of you who know the story know that a great deal of work went into that relationship. But love was not enough for this deaf mute child. After those nonspecific factors set the stage, there was the teaching of a new cognitive map for the universe, a map that reorganized the entire world of her experience in a most exciting way, that affected areas far removed from the original learning. That is a metaphor for successful therapy. Unfortunately it may also suggest the rarity with which that degree of success is attained, the effort, the skill, the devotion, the involvement that's required and the weakness of our theories in explaining how it happens.

NOTES

Freud, S. Analysis terminable and interminable. *International Journal of Psychoanalysis*, 1937, *18*, 373-405.

Index

accomplices, 8
Ackerman, N. W., 8
acting out, 69-70, 76, 113
aggression, 71
agoraphobia, 75
Alcoholics Anonymous, 91
alcoholism, 20
alcohol related problems, 23
Alexander, Franz, 98, 101
ambition, 126, 127
American Psychiatric Association, 2
analyst-patient relationship, 68, 70-71, 73, 104; analyzing the process, 121; corrective emotional experience, 70-71; importance of, 143-46; interpersonal relationship, 44-45
anger, 107
anti-social behavior, 23
anxiety, 19, 24, 38, 50, 106-8, 111, 124
Arlow, Jacob A., 91
assumptions, maladaptive, 15-16, 17-18
assumptive world, 36, 39
authoritarian therapists, 104-5
autonomy, 150-51

Balint, Michael, 78, 79, 102

behavior(s): anti-social, 23; compulsive, 111, 113, 116; masochistic, 109; obsessive-compulsive, 140; passive-agressive, 23; theories of, 105-8
behavioral changes, 6
behavior therapy, 18, 22-23, 146
Bell, N. W., 8
Benedek, T., 7
bereavement, 122
Blanck, W., 7
Bowen, M., 8
brain disease, 104
brainwashing, 89-90
Brenner, Charles, 95
Breuer, Josef, 83

change, 141-44; behavioral, 6; definitive, 44-45; facilitative, 44; internal, 6-7; intrapsychic, 31, 33; models of, 142; nature of, 43-44
child-parent relationship, see parent-child relationship
cognitive therapy, 18, 22-23
communication, 104, 144, 147; disturbances in, 15; marital, 5; nonverbal, 93, 104; symbolic, 17
compliance, social, 7
compulsive behavior, 111, 113, 116

About the Editor and Contributors

EDITOR

J. Martin Myers, M.D., formerly Psychiatrist-in-Chief, is presently Psychiatrist-in-Residence and Chairman of the Continuing Education Operating Committee at The Institute of Pennsylvania Hospital, Philadelphia. He is also Professor of Clinical Psychiatry at the University of Pennsylvania, School of Medicine.

A past president of the American College of Psychiatrists, he has been long active in educational programs for medical students, psychiatric residents, and practicing psychiatrists as well as clinical and administrative psychiatry with publications in these areas.

Dr. Myers received his A.B. from Princeton University, M.D. from Johns Hopkins University, and his psychiatric training at the Johns Hopkins Hospital.

CONTRIBUTORS

Paul Dewald, M.D., is Clinical Professor of Psychiatry, School of Medicine, St. Louis University and Medical Director of the St. Louis Psychoanalytic Institute. He has been very active in teaching, supervision, and practice of psychoanalysis and individual psychotherapy. He has authored several books, book chapters, and many journal articles on these topics.

Jerome D. Frank, M.D., Ph.D., is Professor-Emeritus of Psychiatry, School of Medicine, Johns Hopkins University, where he has been active in research on the effectiveness of group and individual psychotherapy. His book *Persuasion and Healing*, published by Johns Hopkins Press in 1973, has become a classic for those interested in the psychotherapeutic process.

Jerry M. Lewis, M.D., is Psychiatrist-in-Chief of the Timberlawn Psychiatric Hospital, Director of Research of the Timberlawn Foundation and Clinical Professor of Psychiatry, Family Practice, and Community Medicine, Southwestern Medical School of the University of Texas at Dallas. His book and journal publications have been numerous and about psychotherapy and family dynamics.

Robert Michels, M.D., is the Barklie McKee Henry Professor and Chairman, Department of Psychiatry, Cornell University and Psychiatrist-in-Chief of the New York Hospital. He is a training and supervising analyst of the Columbia University Center of Psychoanalytic Training and Research. He has written numerous publications, particularly on psychiatric education, psychoanalysis, ethical and social issues.

Paul Ornstein, M.D., is Professor of Psychiatry, College of Medicine, University of Cincinnati; Training and Supervising Psychoanalyst, Cincinnati Psychoanalytic Institute. Among other publications, he is editor of the two volume *The Search for the Self — Selected Writings of Heinz Kohut* published by International Universities Press, 1978.

Leon Salzman, M.D., is Professor of Clinical Psychiatry, Georgetown University Medical School in Washington where he is in private practice. His training included both the Washington School of Psychiatry and the Washington-Baltimore Psychoanalytic Institute. His publications — books, book chapters, journal articles — focus especially on treatment of obsessive-compulsives.

Alan Z. Skolnikoff, M.D., is Associate Clinical Professor, Department of Psychiatry, University of California, San Francisco and a training and supervising analyst, San Francisco Psychoanalytic Institute. He has been actively involved in research of the psychoanalytic process with others at San Francisco Psychoanalytic Institute and of brief therapy of stress response syndromes at the Center for the Study of Neurosis.